THE WINEMAKER'S DICTIONARY

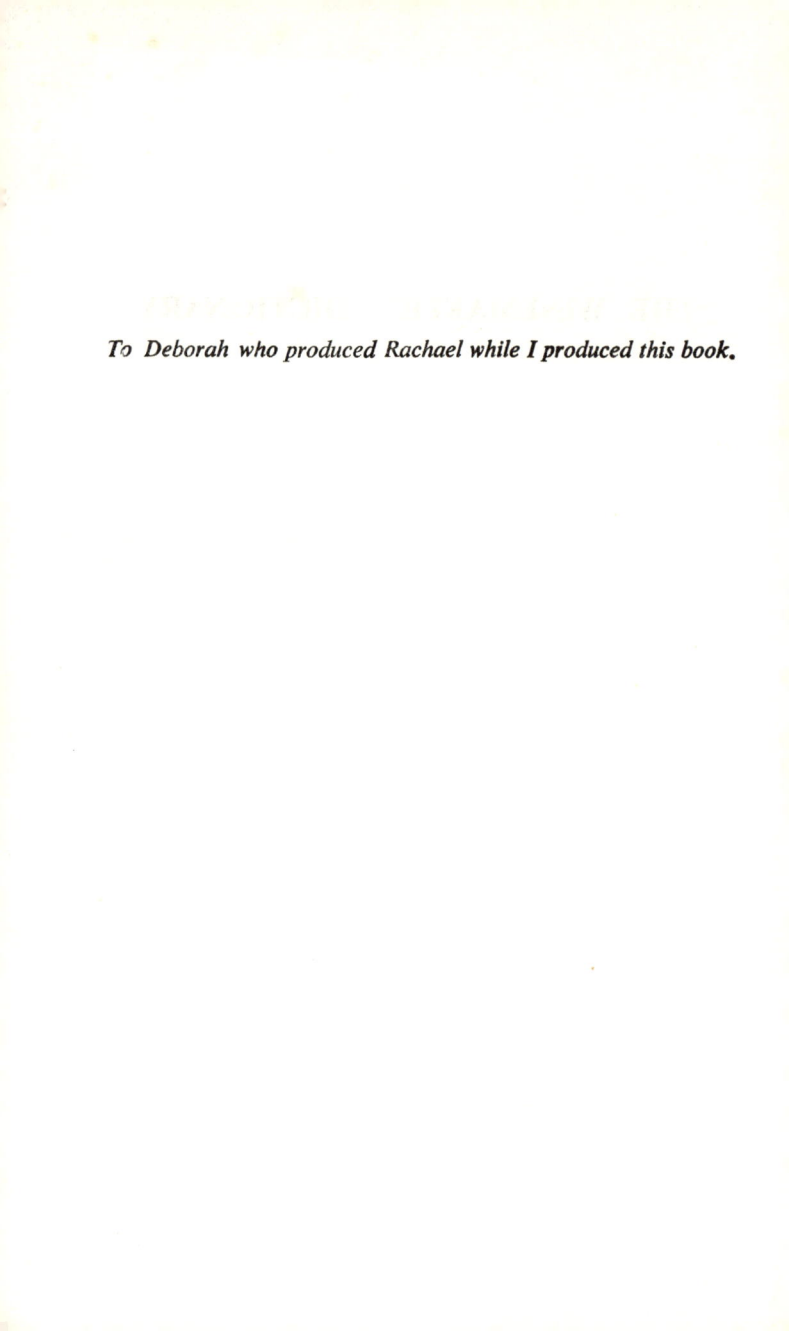

To Deborah who produced Rachael while I produced this book.

THE WINEMAKER'S DICTIONARY

by

PETER McCALL

THE WINEMAKER'S DICTIONARY

Peter McCall 1974

© *"The Amateur Winemaker" Publications Ltd.* 1975

I SBN 0 900841 37 0

Printed in Great Britain by;
Standard Press, (Andover) Ltd.
South Street, Andover

1st IMPRESSION 1974
2nd IMPRESSION 1975
3rd IMPRESSION 1976
4th IMPRESSION 1978
5th IMPRESSION 1980

Published by;
The Amateur Winemaker Publications Ltd,
South Street, Andover, Hants. SP10 2BU.

PREFACE

When we started making our own wines and beers we were bewildered by the profusion of books available to the amateur winemaker. Needless to say, *First Steps* was the first book. Progressing from this there is quite a gap in the standard of books, particularly in the depth of language that is met with. Thus a book will explain a term fully, but may take several pages to do so. All the while talking in this strange language of winemaking—could it be called Vignerol?—and for tyros like ourselves there is no *First Steps* type of definition. Nor is it always easy to find, without a library of winemaking and a good cross-indexing system, summaries of meanings.

Lest we be misunderstood, let it be known we do not mean, nor intend to imply, any criticism of those experts who have been our teachers. It is merely that we require for ourselves a simple answer to our queries.

The idea for this book came while looking up some comparatively simple topic which, nonetheless, took some twenty pages of scattered reading in several books. Thus the object of this book is to present the terms, chemicals, ingredients and techniques encountered in winemaking in the most logical form possible—alphabetical—as concisely as possible.

Whilst meant for winemakers such as ourselves—not much more than starters—it is to be hoped that the expert will not cast too disparaging an eye upon it, and may even find it of value!

Most entries may appear at first sight to be incomplete, but our aim has been that each entry contains only the essentials of that topic. Therefore you will find that we do not explain every term on each occasion it occurs. Instead, by looking up that word and using the cross-references provided, the voids are, we hope, filled. As may be your glasses!

ACKNOWLEDGEMENTS

I should like to record my thanks to the following for help in the compilation of this book:

M. Jean Barnier, of Générac, Nîmes.

Mrs. Pamela Vandyke Price, for permission to use her definition of corked wine.

Dr. W. Honneyman, for permission to quote from his pamphlet, *Calculating Alcohol Yields*.

The Clarendon Press, Oxford, for permission to quote from *The Shorter Oxford Dictionary*.

The firms too numerous to mention individually who helped with technical data on their products.

Mrs. M. T. Rodway, for typing the manuscript; and Messrs. S. R. C. Johnson, A. McCall and A. McK. Nicholl for reading and correcting it.

— A —

Accidents The euphemistic term used to cover a wide range of mishaps, from trivial to disastrous, during the making of wines. Common faults in wines are infections, wrong colours and hazes. For methods of determining the cause of the trouble. (See Diagnosis; and Tests).

Acetaldehyde is the second member of the aldehyde group. It is formed during fermentation from pyruvic acid by the enzyme carboxylase. It is an essential step in alcohol production, since no alcohol is produced unless acetaldehyde is reduced by the enzyme zymase. Large doses of sulphite will inhibit its reduction to alcohol so that glycerol will be the main product. If the fermentation temperature is too high, or infection occurs, an oxidation reaction takes place and acetic acid is produced rather than alcohol. This may also happen if a wine is over oxygenated during racking. However, bisulphite will combine with the acetaldehyde to prevent this oxidation reaction. Hence the need for bisulphite at racking. (See Fermentation Pathways, Appendices IX and X)

Acetals are chemical compounds formed by the joining of an alcohol and an aldehyde, characterised by having a pleasant aromatic odour. They are formed during maturation, and play an important part in the bouquet of a wine.

Acetamide is a chemical substance which, if present in a wine, will cause an unpleasant off flavour usually referred to as *mousey*. It is produced by some of the spoilage bacteria and, once present, there is no cure. Prevention is by scrupulous hygiene at all stages of wine production.

Acetate, Ethyl The ester of acetaldehyde and ethyl alcohol, having a smell like that of pear drops. It is usually formed during the spoilage of a wine and its conversion to vinegar.

Acetic Acid is a monobasic organic acid. It is formed in small amounts during fermentation and is the principal constituent of vinegar. Wine which is exposed to the air will become infected by bacteria which may cause the oxidation of alcohol to acetaldehyde and then to acetic acid. Wine which has become infected first shows an oily sheen on its surface and eventually smells vinegary and sour. It is interesting to note that during ageing small amounts of acetic acid are formed by oxidation of ethyl alcohol, without spoilage occurring. Indeed, its presence in small amounts adds to the final quality of the wine.

Acetification A term for the oxidation of alcohol to acetic acid. When this occurs it is best to allow the wine to go completely to vinegar. If this is not desired the wine must be thrown away lest it be the cause of further infection in the winery.

Acetifying Bacteria are the species of bacteria responsible for the acetification of wine. They gain access to the wine by failure in hygiene. Commonly, this infection is carried by the fruit fly Drosophila.

Acetobacter One of two groups of bacteria responsible for the acetification of wine by oxidising the alcohol to acetic acid. (See Acetomonas)

Acetoin is a substance produced by lactobacilli in addition to lactic acid. It produces its own characteristic off flavour. Prevention of this spoilage substance is by hygiene at all stages of production.

Acetomonas The second group of acetifying bacteria. The first (*acetobacter*) oxidise the alcohol to acetic acid which is then broken down to water and carbon dioxide by the action of acetomonas.

Acid Chemical compounds characterised by the presence of a free hydrogen ion which in solution separates or dissociates from the other radicals to be available for reduction reactions. Acids are either strong or weak and form salts if they are mixed with alkalis.

Acidity is a wide topic with many important facets to the winemaker. To discuss these under one general heading would make too long an entry to extract short amounts of information, and so the various aspects of the subject have been treated separately under their respective headings.

Acids, Amino, are naturally occurring weak acids which join together in long chains to form proteins. They all contain nitrogen and may be a source of some of the nitrogenous material necessary for yeast growth, for they, like humans, need protein. Unless alternative nitrogen sources are available to the yeast amino acids may be de-aminated and fusel oils produced, with consequential loss of yeast growth and possibly a stuck ferment. During autolysis, amino acids are released into the wine with adverse effects on taste and bouquet, except in the case of champagne and sherry, where it is a required feature of production that the wine rests on the lees during maturation.

Acid Mixture   See Mixture of Acids.

Acid, Plant,   Another name for organic acids found in green vegetables where they play an important part in the Krebs' cycle (the name for the series of chemical reactions that occur during plant respiration). They are weak acids—they do not dissociate completely in solution—and play an important part in wine making. (See Acid Types, Bouquet, Esters).

Acid Reduction   If after initial assay of the must the acidity is too high, there are three ways of reducing it:

(a) **Dilution**   The acidity of the must is assayed and expressed as acidity per gallon. If, for example, the acidity of 1 pint of juice is 64 parts per thousand (p.p.t.), then the acidity per gallon will be 8 p.p.t. If an acidity of 4 p.p.t. is required, the juice is diluted by one volume.

(b) **Chalk**   can be added in the form of *Precipitated Calcium Carbonate*. ¼ oz. per gallon will reduce the acidity by about 1·5 p.p.t. Care must be taken during this operation as foaming will occur.

(c) **Bentonite,**   used as a fining agent will reduce the acidity. This is because bentonite joins with tannin before clearing a wine and it is this conjoined tannin which is removed with a resultant reduction of acidity.

Acid, Stock Solution Because of the difficulty of accurately weighing small quantities of additives for a must a stock solution can be prepared containing a known weight per unit volume; i.e. if a solution is prepared containing 1 oz (= 30 gms approx.) in 500 mls, then 20 ml will contain approximately 1 gm. (See Mixture of acids.)

Acid, Strong Hydrochloric, Nitric or Sulphuric acids. Of no interest to the amateur winemaker except as a unit of acidity. Free acidity is expressed in units of sulphuric acid, and measured in Parts per Thousand of that acid in Europe. In the USA tartaric acid is used as the unit. (See Appendix I).

Acid Taste in excess in a wine will give it tartness and tend to drown other characteristics. The presence of free, or titratable, acid is important to give zest to a wine.

Acid Taste and Acidity are obviously related, but the acidity as measured by titration and as detected by the palate do not always agree, since a sweet wine with the same acidity as a dry wine will not taste as acid due to the masking of the acid by the unfermented sugar.

Acid Types The acids met with in winemaking are listed and their properties and functions discussed in the respective entry:

Acetic	Formic	Oxalic	Tannic
Butyric	Lactic	Propionic	Tartaric
Citric	Malic	Succinic	Volatile
Ellagic			

Acid, Weak See acid plant; and under various types and Buffers.

Acidity The wife's reaction to the taking over of the kitchen for wine making!

Acidity, Correction of Most musts prepared by amateur wine makers are not of the right acidity unless corrected. Having decided on the required acidity of the wine the wine is titrated against Sodium Hydroxide and the weight of free acid determined. By subtracting the desired acidity from the actual acid present the amount of acid required for correction is obtained. If a negative result is obtained the must needs to be reduced in acid.

Acidity Determination 10 mls of wine are diluted three or four fold with distilled water. Either phenolphthalein, or B.D.H. Universal Indicator, is added and decinormal Sodium Hydroxide run into the beaker until the end point is reached. The amount of alkali required to neutralise the acid in the wine is divided by 2 to give the free acid of the must in Parts per Thousand of Sulphuric acid. Sulphuric acid is not actually used in winemaking but is employed as the unit of measurement or standard for the purpose of assessing acidity; it is merely a convenient international method of expressing the quantity or weight of acid present as if it were Sulphuric acid itself.

Acidity of Fruits varies from year to year. Generally speaking, the acidity and sugar content of the fruit are in inverse proportion. A good summer will mean 'sweet' fruit with a low acid content.

Acidity and Maturing A wine with an acid content at the upper limit for its type or style will take longer to mature, but once ready for drinking will have a better bouquet than a less acid wine (due to the greater amounts of esters formed during maturation). Citric does not readily esterify, but malic and, even more so, succinic acids combine with alcohol to form bouquet producing esters. It must be emphasised that, for these changes to occur, time is essential, and that a wine drunk young will show no improvement in bouquet over the 'natural' bouquet from the ingredients.

Acidity of Musts is the free acidity present in the must after preparation. Its correct value is important in producing a well balanced, rounded wine. For usual ranges see Appendix II.

Acidity, Role of The benefits obtained from *correct* acid balance are, taking them in their chronological order:
   (a) **Bacteriocidal and -static** Most of the spoilage organisms are killed or inhibited by free acid. Those that are

not killed by the acid will not become well established, and those surviving will be killed by the alcohol produced. (Alcohol is one of the best antiseptics.)

(b) **Stimulation of Fermentation** is aided by the presence of citric acid.

(c) **Glycerol Formation** is stimulated by the presence of adequate tartaric acid.

(d) **Ester Formation** is aided by the presence of malic and succinic acids.

(e) **Balanced Taste** is a function of many things, but one of the most important in quality wines is the acidity. Too low an acidity will produce an insipid wine; too high, an acidic wine.

(f) **Keeping Qualities** are enhanced by an adequate acidity, ensuring a mature wine without spoilage; a balanced wine without off flavours.(See mixture of acids)

Acidity, Titratable is that part of the acids present which can be measured by titration against Sodium Hydroxide.

Acidity, Tolerance of Bacteria to See Bacteria and Acidity.

Acidity, Tolerance of Yeast to See Yeast, Tolerance to Acidity.

Acidity of Wine Types depends on the wine style desired and suggested ranges are given in the table in the appendix II.

Actinic Action of Sunlight The colour of many wines, especially Rosés, is not stable, and may undergo alteration when exposed to sunlight. Frequently the bleached colour is most unattractive and therefore some means of shading is necessary, such as fermenting in dark jars or under opaque sheeting (such as black polythene bags), and bottling in coloured glass. Much Rosé wine is sold commercially in clear glass, principally to exhibit the attractive colour; these wines are known to be reasonably stable.

"Activating" Yeast is to prepare the yeast for addition to the must by making a Starter.

Activity Where the action is. Either in a fermenting must, or in the kitchen, tidying up before one's wife gets back!

Additives Any chemical or compound added to the must, other than the basic recipe ingredients. They are essential for peace of mind for, if lacking, there is the possibility that the fermentation will stick. Basically, additives are necessary foodstuffs for yeast growth or yeast enzyme activity which will ensure a healthy ferment with minimum amounts of fusel oils being produced. (See Dilution and Nutrients).

Additives, Amounts required.

	per gal
Ammonium phosphate *or* ammonium sulphate	5 gms
Potassium phosphate *or* potassium sulphate ...	2 gms
Magnesium sulphate	0·5 gms
Vitamin B_1	3 mgm

Adjusting Either raising or lowering the acidity or specific gravity of a must to the required level.

Aeration is to stir a must in the presence of air to ensure the dissolving of oxygen in the mixture so that the first stage of fermentation, the establishment of a healthy yeast colony, can take place.

Aerobic Fermentation Before alcoholic fermentation can commence, aerobic fermentation (or fermentation in the presence of air) takes place to establish a healthy yeast colony. During this phase no alcohol is formed. Aerobic fermentation, once an adequate yeast colony has been established, is not desirable for, apart from the lack of alcohol formed in the presence of air, there is always the possibility of infection.

Agar A special jelly for growing cultures which the amateur winemaker may come across if he buys his yeast in the form of agar slopes. Agar is placed in test tubes and yeast grown upon the agar under sterile conditions. When required, the yeast is activated in the usual manner. Agar is a polysaccharide derived from seaweed.

Ageing A complex series of oxidation, reduction an desterification reactions which take place in the dark still waters of the cask or bottle long after fermentation has ceased (as long as the wine still survives for this to happen!). The subject is fully discussed under maturation and its related headings.

Air Lock As a first line defence against spoilage and as an easy means of determining if fermentation is in progress, the air lock in probably the simplest, yet most essential, piece of equipment for the winemaker.

Air Space The gap above the wine in the maturation jar. This should, unless making a sherry, be only ¼ inch, when it needs to be about ¼ of the jar. The space between cork and wine in the bottle should be about ½ inch. (See Ullage).

Airing Cupboard (or Linen Closet, to U.S. readers) A good place to keep the must during the primary fermentation. For the winemaker who "has everything", a fermentation cupboard is better. American and Canadian readers will prefer their heated basements.

Albumin A protein complex commonly found on the breakfast table as the white of your morning egg. In wine making this part of the egg is used for fining wine.

Albuminous Protein Animal proteins used for fining wines. The commonly used sorts are either ox blood or egg white. They react with tannin to form an insoluble complex which will precipitate out of solution. The drawback to their use is the large volume of wine a small quantity of fresh albumen will clear. If available, dried albumen will overcome the problem, because small amounts can be accurately weighed, whereas it is rather difficult to divide an egg into fiftieths!

Alcohol The object of the exercise!

Alcohol, Amyl See Amyl Alcohol.

Alcohol, Colour Extraction by Pigments present in the skins of many red fruits are insoluble in water. However, they are soluble in alcohol so that pulp fermentation will result in the extraction of colour as alcohol is gradually produced. Once the desired depth of colour is obtained the fruit pulp is removed from the fermentation vat.

Alcohol Dehydrogenase is an enzyme found in the liver of man. It is the enzyme chiefly responsible for the metabolism of alcohol. Recently it has been hypothesised that this enzyme is lacking in persons suffering from alcoholism; thus suggesting that alcoholism is less an addiction resulting from intemperance than an organic disease; an opinion held by many for some time. It is a sobering thought that soon the alcoholic may benefit from treatment in much the same way as a diabetic.

Alcohol Determination as performed by the professional winemaker is a complex expensive business involving special equipment. For the amateur, an approximation may be obtained by dividing the total gravity drop by 7·5 (or slightly more accurately by reference to the table of dividing factors). Better still, if the equipment is available, is to measure accurately 200 mls of wine of a known specific gravity and to boil it down to about half its volume to drive off the alcohol. It is then made up to its original volume with distilled water and the S.G. taken again. The RISE in S.G. is deducted from 1000: 0·16 is added to the result as a correction. The resultant spirit indication gives the alcohol content by reference to tables.(See Appendix IV).

Alcohol and Diabetes See Diabetes.

Alcohol, Ethyl The second of the primary alcohols. It is produced naturally by the fermentation of sugars by yeasts. When an amateur winemaker talks about alcohol, it is ethyl alcohol he means. It is easily mixed with water and when diluted has a not unpleasant taste, although in a wine an alcoholic taste is not aimed for. It is lighter than water, and this fact is made use of when employing the hydrometer.

Alcohol, Higher Alcohols with long carbon chains are toxic and therefore undesirable in a wine. They are formed if there is not a high enough concentration of free nitrogen for yeast growth by the de-amination of amino acids. Produced only in small amounts in normal fermentation, they are called fusel oils.

Alcohol, Medicinal Properties As well as being the pleasantest night sedation, it is essentially non-addictive. It is a good vaso-dilator (it helps the circulation). Unfortunately, the Minister of Health excluded it from the list of prescribable drugs, so that its medical uses are academic unless you go out and buy another bottle! It is interesting to note that whisky or brandy is a safer, cheaper, less addictive night sedation than most tablets normally prescribed. It is not a stimulant, as thought by most people, but rather a depressant; hence the Breathalyser and laws about drinking and driving.

Alcohol, Methyl is the first of the alcohols. It is formed from the breakdown of pectin to galactonuric acid and methyl alcohol. Although toxic, in the concentrations it is found in wine it is not harmful and adds character and roundness to a wine. It is NOT a product of fermentation. If drunk, as by 'Meths' drinkers, it will cause blindness, liver and brain damage and, eventually, death. Therefore, stick to 'Ethyl'.

Alcohol Potential The alcohol concentration expected from fermentation if it continues to dryness. This is estimated from the starting gravity. (See Appendix IV(a)).

Alcohol and Reduction in Volume Due to the affinity alcohol and water have for each other, there is a contraction in volume when the two are mixed together. Thus one pint each of alcohol and water results in slightly less than two pints when mixed.

Alcohol and Sterilisation Once the effect of sulphite added prior to fermentation has worn off, the must relies on acidity and the formation of alcohol to protect it against infection. There are very few bacteria that can survive in alcoholic media. Any wild yeasts that may survive sulphiting will be killed by an alcohol concentration of about 4 per cent.

Alcohol Strength Is synonymous with alcoholic concentration, and can be varied by the selection of the starting gravity. In commercial wines this usually varies between 8 per cent and 14 per cent.

Alcohol, Tolerance of Yeast to One of the cardinal properties of a good yeast is that it will not be inhibited until high levels of alcohol have been achieved. It may be possible to exceed the normal tolerance point by feeding the yeast with small amounts of sugar at intervals throughout fermentation, rather than adding all the sugar at the start. Most yeasts will produce 12 per cent to 14 per cent alcohol by volume, although with care 18 per cent can be achieved.

Alcohol Yield from Fermentation is related to the total fermentable base and the alcohol tolerance of the yeast. It does not usually exceed 14 per cent, although 18 per cent can be obtained with careful control of fermentation.

Aldehyde A group of chemical compounds characterised by the presence of a –CHO radical. The aldehyde of prime importance to the winemaker is acetaldehyde.

Aldose A portmanteau word to describe one of the main groups of sugars. They are characterised by having an aldehyde group (hence the Ald- part of their name); the –OSE is a suffix to denote a monosaccharide. Glucose is the aldose of winemaking import.

Alloy Capsules See Capsules, Alloy.

Alkali A chemical compound which, when mixed with an acid, forms water and salts. If hydrochloric acid and sodium hydroxide are mixed, then sodium chloride and water are obtained. When determining the free acidity of a wine an alkali, sodium hydroxide, is added and titrated against the free acid. In this case the products are water and the sodium salts of the acids present in the wine.

Aluminium Containers made from aluminium are, other than those made from stainless steel, the safest for boiling winemaking ingredients, but do not leave highly acidic liquids in lengthy contact with aluminium vessels, and do not ferment or store in them.

Amines A group of chemicals produced by some of the spoilage organisms. They are characterised by having a fishy smell.

Amino–Acids See Acids, Amino.

Ammonium Phosphate Most amateur musts are lacking in the nitrogen necessary for yeast growth. If no other source is available amino-acids from dead yeast will be de-aminated with the result that fusel oils will be produced as a by-product. The phosphate radical is also of great importance for a healthy vigorous fermentation as it is required in some of the reactions as an energy transferer. About 5 gms per gallon are required, together with other additives.

Ammonium Sulphate A certain amount of the sulphate radical is obtained from bisulphite added to the must. If the water is hard there will usually be enough sulphate present, unless making sherry. If, however, the pH of the water is too alkaline then sulphate can play a useful role in the lowering of pH. The major role of ammonium sulphate is the nitrogen it makes available for yeast growth. However, the sulphate is also needed for synthesis of some proteins.

Amyl Alcohol is an important by-product of fermentation, formed chiefly by de-amination of amino acids. A small amount may also be formed from sugars. Amyl alcohol has several isomeric forms. Normally present in low concentrations, it will, in higher concentrations, change an otherwise good wine into a harsh tasting, unpleasant smelling beverage, with possible toxic effects. It may also inhibit the fermentation pathways if present in more than trace amounts. In 'normal' low concentrations it helps confer bouquet to a wine.

Amylase The enzyme which breaks down starch to maltose and short chain dextrins. The short chain dextrins are broken down by maltase to glucose. If amylase is not added to a starch containing must the finished wine will have a haze due to the starch and dextrins, since wine yeasts do not secrete this enzyme.

Anaerobic Fermentation is fermentation taking place in the absence of air. Under such conditions yeast does not (as we should) die, but instead, being a facultative anaerobe, continues to flourish and, as a by-product (to the yeast) or as an object (to us), alcohol is produced. Reproduction does still take place, but at a much slower rate. The yeast will not survive for ever even assuming a limitless supply of sugar and nutrients, but as the alcohol level rises it kills the yeast cells by denaturing the enzymes.

Analysis The examination of a substance or mixture for its constituents and their quantities. This should be routinely carried out on musts and wines for their acidity, sugar content,

S.G., and, if indicated, possible contaminants causing hazes or faults. (See Test Entries).

Aneurine-hydrochloride The chemical name given to one of the B vitamins. Yeasts, in common with all other living organisms, need vitamins for reproduction. Although all animals can produce a certain amount of the vitamins they require, they still have to include some in their diet. 3 mg per gallon is a generally accepted dose; it is easily obtained from any chemist in tablet form.

Anthocyanins are a group of related plant pigments (either red, blue or purple) which combine with glucose to form glycosides. In the plant, depending on soil pH, neighbours may vary widely in colour such is the effect of pH on colour production. Glycosides are often bitter to taste and some of them, such as the foxglove glycoside digitalis, can be toxic unless taken as the doctor prescribes! If released, usually by alcoholic extraction, they will add colour to a must. (See Extraction by Alcohol).

Anthoxanthins A class of plant pigments which are yellow in colour.

Anti-Oxidant A term for any chemical used to prevent oxidation in wine, usually at racking time. See Ascorbic Acid; Sulphite; Ethyl pyrocarbonate.

Aperitif The generic name for wines and other alcoholic beverages (with the exception of beer) consumed before meals with a view to stimulation of the appetite. They are usually more palatable than medically prescribed tonics, and frequently more effective!

Apiculate Yeasts are so called because of their shape; they are pointed at both ends. They are found in profusion on most fruits. They are undesirable in winemaking because they are not wine yeasts and, like all yeasts, they are capable of fermentation, but will only produce 3 to 4 per cent alcohol before being inhibited by the alcohol they have produced. They tend to ferment rapidly to their end point, and will produce a sweet cordial rather than a wine. If a must is not sterilised, apiculate, or wild yeasts, may commence fermentation but, with the other organisms present on the fruit, spoilage will almost inevitably occur. (See Yeast entries).

Apo-Ferment This is a complex protein substance present in all living cells which select the type of compound to be metabolised by the coferment.

Arabinose One of the pentose sugars. It is effectively not fermented by yeasts and, therefore, if available, can be of use as a sweetening agent.

Argols Tartaric acid tends to form potassium tartrate. As it is not very soluble it tends to produce a haze in a wine. Cooling the wine decreases its solubility so that it precipitates out. The precipitate may then crystallise to form crystals often referred to as Argols. The free acidity of the wine will be lowered considerably if excess potassium salts are present in the must, either as potassium bisulphite or as potassium phosphate.

Aroma See Bouquet.

Artificial Sweeteners See Lactose; Potassium Sorbate; Saccharin.

Asbestos A mineral of value as a fining agent. Asbestos pulp is prepared and wine filtered through it. There is a danger of contaminating the wine and producing an asbestos taste; also it tends to remove some of the wine flavour due to its absorptive action. Care must be taken when using it as it can be a health hazard. It is well known as the cause of one of the pneumoconioses, a lung disease, and has not yet been cleared from causing trouble in other organs. This is, however, unlikely in the amounts used by the amateur winemaker and is, indeed, present in the commercial beers we drink when we run out of our own! The government has surveyed the situation and said that it is safe in the quantities present in beer after fining.

Ascomycetes One of the four classes into which the true fungi are divided. In addition to exotics like the Truffle, this class also includes beer and wine yeasts.

Aqua Vitae A general term for strong spirituous liquors, derived from their previous medicinal use as stimulants.

Ascorbic Acid is a strong anti-oxidant and can be used instead of bisulphite at racking time to prevent over-oxidation. If it is used, it must be remembered that it will raise the acidity of the wine. Some commercial vignerons use it in the production of wines which are high in malic acid. It is not bacteriocidal, so that after racking, a malo-lactic fermentation can be encouraged to change the malic acid to lactic and thereby smooth the wine.

Ascorbic Acid & Sulphite are best used together in the ratio of one part sulphite to four parts ascorbic acid: i.e. 30 ppm sulphite and 500mg/gallon ascorbic acid. In this way, one gets the combined anti-oxidation effect as well as effective anti-bacterial protection, without the risk of bottle stink.

Aspergillus A mould sometimes encountered in winemaking when a prepared must does not start immediately and becomes infected by aerobic spores. Aspergillus may be recognised by its characteristic black colour. If infection does occur it is possible to save the wine by straining the must and restarting. In Japan, however, it is required to make Saké. A prophet is not without honour!

Astringency A wine-tasting term to describe dryness of the mouth on tasting a wine. If pronounced and unpleasant, it may be due to excess tannin.

Australian Honey Honey is a good source of sugar and owes its character to the presence of floral esters and pollens, which will have more effect upon any wine made with it than cane sugar. Honey will help in the production of a smooth wine, but is nearly always detectable, so its use is double-edged in quality wines. Care must be exercised with honey from Australia in case it contains any eucalyptus, which will confer a bitter taste to the wine or mead.

Autolysis When yeast cells die, the cell, no longer protected by the electrical charge on the cell membrane is metabolised and broken down by the enzyme systems of the yeast itself. The whole series of complex reactions is known as autolysis (or self destruction).

— B —

Bacillus Butyricus One of the spoilage organisms which may cause its characteristic off-smell like rancid butter if allowed access to wine due to poor hygiene. If this occurs, the wine should be discarded.

Bacteria are micro-organisms abounding everywhere, ranging in properties from beneficial to fatal. Luckily for the winemaker the disease-causing 'bugs' do not infect his wine. Bacteria are, due to their abundance, *de facto*, present in virtually all winemaking ingredients. Unless care is taken first to kill or neutralise and then to exclude further infection, this is exactly what will occur, with catastrophic results for the wine. Bacteria are, broadly speaking, divided into two types, aerobic and anaerobic, and the infections or spoilage due to the bacteria differ accordingly. A well-prepared must, being high in sugar, nutrients and salts, provides a rich culture medium for bacteria and explains their predilection for wines.

Bacteria, Acetifying are present on all rotting fruit, so sound fruit is the first step to a non-acetic wine. An uncovered must, due to the presence of sugar and fermentation, will attract the fruit fly which, as a carrier of acetifying bacteria, will cause the change of wine to vinegar, and therefore all wines, no matter what stage they are in, must be covered.

Bacteria and Acidity A must which has an adequate acidity to achieve a balanced wine will have, in general, an acidity sufficient to kill or inhibit bacteria. However, wines being complex buffer systems, the titratable acidity is not a guarantee of a low enough pH to control infection. A pH of between 3 and 4 at the start of fermentation will prevent infection. The usual range of titratable acidities lies between 4 and 8, depending on wine style.

Bacteria, Aerobic These spoilage bacteria require air to survive and multiply so that, once a must has been sterilised, protection from access of air and airborne bacteria is essential, either by an air lock or polythene sheeting over the fermentation vat. The blanket of carbon dioxide over an active ferment will do much to prevent the entry of aerobes but, once the ferment slows, the danger is real and requires careful attention to hygiene and exclusion of air. Usually infection can be suspected if a haze accompanied by an off flavour develops. If tests for infection are positive the wine should be sterilised with sulphite and, after racking, restarted.

Bacteria and Alcohol Bacteria not killed by sulphite are killed by alcohol in fairly low concentrations. Those surviving initial sulphiting will be killed by the alcohol of fermentation. If fermentation is delayed it will allow inhibited bacteria time to re-establish themselves.

Bacteria, Anaerobic These bacteria thrive in the absence of air and, therefore, unlike aerobes, need more than exclusion of air for prevention of troubles. They are, however, killed by sulphite and therefore the use of this at racking times will prevent them getting a foothold, presuming a hygienic fermentation. Lactobacilli responsible for the malo-lactic reaction, are, under controlled conditions, beneficial anti-aerobes. (See Ascorbic Acid).

Bacteria, Haze due to See Haze, bacterial.

Bacteria and Heat All bacteria are killed by high temperatures; so for equipment this is the best sterilising method, if made of glass! Heat is of use for certain types of ingredient which can be boiled safely.

Bacteria, Lactic Acid are the main anaerobic bacteria the winemaker will come across.

Bacteria, Lactic Acid and Malo-Lactic Fermentation If, at bottling time, the wine is not sulphited, a slightly sparkling wine may be produced. This is due to the action of the lactobacilli which, at this stage of the wine, break down malic acid to lactic acid and, in the process, give off carbon dioxide—this causes the sparkle. This reaction is aimed for in some commercial wines. The end result of the reaction is a less acid wine, due to the less acid taste of lactic compared to malic acid.

Bacteria, Lactic Acid and Ropiness Some of the lactobacilli species multiply and stick together forming long chains which can be seen in the wine. Due to the mucus the bacteria secrete on their surface, the wine becomes thick and oily. Prevention is by hygiene and the cure, if needed, is to sulphite the wine, stir it thoroughly to break up the chains, and allow the wine to settle before filtering. Usually there is no associated off-flavour developed with this condition and, once treated, the wine should be drunk soon after filtering.

Bacteria, Lactic Acid and Spoilage Some of the lactobacilli contain the enzyme lactase, which breaks down sugar to lactic acid and, at the same time, may produce curious off-flavours, usually described as mousey or rancid. They may also produce acetic acid. Their metabolism of sugar to lactic acid will also reduce the potential alcohol yield.

Bacteria and pH Most bacteria can survive only if the pH is between 3 and 7 and this fact may be made use of in hygiene. Therefore, assaying the must prior to pitching the yeast will, in most cases, prevent infection. A starting pH of between 3 and 4 will kill spoilage bacteria whilst not preventing the reproduction of yeast.

Bacteria, Protection against is basically very simple—HYGIENE. At all stages of winemaking, equipment, must or wine are sterilised, or precautions taken against the introduction of infection. The major sterilising agents to the winemaker are: acidity, alcohol, heat, pH and sulphite. After preparation of the must and its sterilisation an air lock is required; at racking sulphite or ascorbic acid are used; and at all stages the equipment is scrupulously cleaned and sterilised before use.

Bacteria Resistance If attempts are made to kill or inhibit bacteria with too low a concentration of sterilising agents there is a danger that the bacteria will not be killed or inhibited, but will instead 'learn' to tolerate that substance. This is *resistance*. The danger exists that the bacteria may actually thrive on the chosen agent, so that its continued use may in fact be dangerous to the cleanliness of the winery. The bacteria may possess the ability to break down the agent (this is common in medicine, but not in winemaking) or it may be able to develop new metabolic pathways.

Bacterial Spoilage   See Infection.

Bacteria and Sulphite   It is no accident that sulphite is the winemaker's major agent against infection; it does not harm fruit and will either kill or neutralise bacteria. At the same time, it does not harm wine yeasts unless in very high concentrations.

Bacteriocidal   is an adjective applied to a substance which has the property of killing bacteria. For winemakers the bacteriocidal agents are sulphite, alcohol and heat.

Bacteriostatic   A term applied to a substance which inhibits the growth of bacteria without necessarily killing them. Such effects may be seen when using too little sulphite. However, some organisms are not killed by sulphite, but they are inhibited from further growth—a static effect, and these are killed by the alcohol as it is formed. Care needs to be taken over the possibility of resistance.

Bad Eggs   The aptly descriptive name given to the smell of hydrogen sulphide.

Baker's Yeast   Although having a reasonable alcohol tolerance of about 12 per cent, it has the property of giving off large volumes of carbon dioxide (which, after all, is what the baker wants!). If used as a wine yeast there will tend to be a rapid frothy ferment which clears slowly and leaves loose, easily disturbed lees. For beginners, the quick ferment is a useful encouragement to further ventures, as it does prove that fermentation occurs even if a superior wine is not produced.

Balance in a Must   A balanced wine is one in which all the taste factors are equal and no single one is dominant, ie the wine is balanced. To achieve this the ingredients, additives and nutrients required to attain this end must be brought together from the beginning in the must, and it is this ability to foresee the taste of a wine in five or six years' time that distinguishes the *ordinaire* from the expert.

Balance for Weighing A beam balance is more accurate for weighing than a spring balance for several reasons, but in winemaking a high degree of accuracy is only needed when measuring the small amounts of additives required and, in these circumstances, a stock solution is the easiest way to accuracy. In normal circumstances, the ordinary kitchen scales are accurate enough for our purposes.

Balling An American scale used in the measurement of Specific Gravity. See Appendix VI.

Bananas for Body The character of bananas in wine is such that if blended into the must at a rate of between ½ and 2 lbs per gallon, depending on the wine style required, the body of the wine will be increased without conferring an obvious banana flavour to it.

Barrels The traditional (and, until recently, the only) storage method for wines and beers. (See Cask entries).

Base A chemical term for a substance which turns litmus blue (i.e., it is alkaline) and also reacts with an acid to form a salt and water. When used of an acid, it refers to the number of hydrogen atoms one molecule of the acid has available for forming hydrogen ions. Thus a dibasic acid has two hydrogen atoms which can dissociate from the molecule.

BDH Universal Indicator A mixture of weak acids which change their colours with changes in pH. By adding a small amount to a sample of unknown pH the green colour of the indicator alters to a shade which varies with the pH. The range of this solution is from pH 3 to 12.

Beet Sugar extracted from the white beet is estimated to be the source of over two-thirds of the household (and winemaking) sugar used today. Chemically, the sugar is as pure as cane sugar, although the French champagne producers claim it confers an earthy flavour if used for chaptalisation.

Bentonite is used for clearing hazes from wines. It is a naturally occurring clay which carries a negative charge. Once this clay is made into a colloidal solution it can attract the positively charged protein and so form larger particles which are too heavy, as well as being electrically neutral, to remain in solution, so that they precipitate out of solution with the result that the wine is cleared of hazes.

Bentonite Gel A proprietary form of bentonite which has the advantage that it is easily put into solution.

Benzene A chemical compound having 6 carbon atoms joined together in a ring structure which, when various radicals are added to it, form many of the compounds encountered in winemaking, eg tannin.

Benzoic Acid As its sodium salt, it is a chemical way of inhibiting fermentation so that, if desired for sweet wines, fermentation does not have to continue to dryness before sweetening the wine to taste.

Berry Round fruit, usually hard, (an exception is the grape which is soft), characterised by having pips or seeds in the centre. They are best crushed and pulp fermented following sterilizing with sulphite. Many of the common berries used for winemaking can be obtained dried and these should be placed in water, sulphited, and pulp fermented. (See Dried Fruit).

Binary Fission One of the methods of reproduction which yeasts can use. It is usually seen in bacteria. In this method of reproduction the cell divides into two similar daughter cells by splitting along a septum which forms in the middle of the cell.

Binning The term used to describe various methods of storing bottles of wine prior to consumption. These vary from bottle racks to arranging the bottles in skilful piles to prevent collapse.

Bins for Bottle Storage are available in varying shapes, sizes and prices, and, dependent on preference and purse, the appropriate choice can be made.

Bisulphite When metabisulphite is added to water it forms bisulphite, and this, after other chemical reactions, results in the liberation of sulphur dioxide gas, *the* winemaking sterilising agent. (See Sulphite entries).

Bitartrate Tartaric acid is a dibasic acid. The argols which may form are, correctly speaking, potassium hydrogen tartrate (only one of the hydrogens is utilised). Potassium bitartrate has potassium atoms attached to both. If this salt forms, it will precipitate out of the wine since it is totally insoluble and, as a result, will lower the acidity. This is unlike potassium tartrate which, being partly soluble, does not precipitate unless low temperatures are applied.

Bitterness A term used to describe the off flavour associated with infection by the lactobacilli which produce mannitol (despite its bitter taste, it is a sugar). Tourne disease is another name given to this condition. Although the infection can be cleared by the use of sulphite, the off flavour arising from the infection is not so easily eradicated and, if blending fails to provide the solution, the wine will have to be discarded.

Bleach, Domestic Provided care is taken to rinse thoroughly with plenty of tap water after use, bleach is an excellent cleaning agent which will remove taints and deposits. In any but the minutest trace it can be toxic and so great care is essential in ensuring its thorough removal from the clean container. (See Quantan Cl).

Blending This is the mixing of ingredients or finished wines to achieve the best possible product. From inception to drinking the aim must be the highest standard, and it is often only by blending that this is possible. (Whether the mixing of grapes or two wines, it is still blending.) Many of the table wines imported from France are the result of blending; and don't forget that champagne is nearly always a blended wine.

Blending for Body Many 'country wines' are made from ingredients that on their own produce thin wines; hence the inclusion in recipes of grape concentrate, raisins or bananas, all of which add to the body of a wine without overpowering the flavour of the main ingredient.

Blending for Bouquet A wine selected to be drunk young will not have time to develop aromatic esters from its own constituents and some vegetables are notoriously lacking in bouquet, even after full maturing. The way out of this impasse is to use flowers, especially rose or elderflower, at the rate of not more than $\frac{1}{2}$ pint of fresh or $\frac{1}{2}$ oz dried flowers added to the must after the first vigorous fermentation has died down. This is to prevent loss of aroma and, for the same reason, flowers should never be boiled. For hock style wines, elderflowers are particularly useful.

Blending Wines As with any blending, the object is to turn a poor wine into a good one! The basic rule with wines is easier than the exercise—select the opposite fault in a second wine, mix the two and the result should be perfection! i.e. A highly astringent wine requires blending with a wine low in tannin. By careful additions (measured) of the low tannin wine, a balance is achieved. Whatever the fault in the wine, the same principle applies.

Blood Commercial vignerons use ox blood as a source of albuminous protein for fining. It reacts with tannin to produce an insoluble precipitate. As well as clearing a wine it will reduce the acidity and astringency.

Bloom on Fruit The dusky sheen on ripe fruit consisting of yeasts (wild as well as wine), moulds and bacteria. Unless washed off and the fruit sterilised, it is these inhabitants of the skin which are one of the causes of infection in wine.

Blue-Fining entails the use of potassium ferrocyanide to remove iron hazes from wine. As ferrocyanide and the compound it forms with iron—ferricyanide—are highly poisonous, *it is NOT an amateur technique.*

Bodega A wine store in Spain, usually above ground for Sherry storage. Sometimes used of a restaurant, or of a **Wine Bar**

Body A tasting term to describe the feel of the wine in the mouth. Wines are usually described as being either full, medium or light bodied. The word may have its roots in the practice (now abandoned) of putting pieces of meat into the vats to "add body".

Body and Bananas See Bananas for Body.

Body, Blending for See Blending for Body.

Body, Grain for An ingredient that is now going out of fashion due to the adverse effect on bouquet and perhaps flavour of a wine, and the abundance of grape concentrate to use in its place. Also, over use of grain may result in excess methyl alcohol being formed which, due to its toxic effects, is to be avoided.

Boiled Water If a water supply is suspected not to be pure (and in the U.K. this is rare) then boiling and cooling prior to use is required. However, in the normal course of events the only effect of boiling water is to drive off the oxygen necessary for establishment of a healthy yeast colony. Because of its ease of use, sulphite is a superior method of sterilising.

Boiling for Extraction See Extraction by Boiling.

Boiling Fruit is limited to dried fruit, and this is to extract as much sugar as possible and to help sterilisation.

Boiling Ingredients Only vegetables and bananas need boiling before pulping and fermenting. This is in order to remove some constituents which if allowed to remain will give a wine a coarse flavour. Do not forget that boiling destroys enzymes, and in this case pectic enzyme will need to be added to prevent hazes, *after the boiled ingredients have cooled.*

Boiling and Sterilising Now that bisulphite is easily and cheaply available, boiling equipment is not necessary. If this method is used, care is needed not to burn oneself, and also to ensure that the equipment, if of plastic, is intended for that sort of heat. With glass, breakage due to thermal shock is not uncommon.

Boiling for Vapourisation Some vegetables contain volatile compounds which, if not driven off by boiling, will spoil the bouquet and flavour of a wine.

Boiling Water is an excellent sterilising agent against many bacteria, but against spore forming bacteria it requires so long a contact time as to become impractical. The best use of boiling water is as an extracting agent when poured over leaves and some fruit and *allowed to cool*. Used in this way, it extracts flavour and sugars and does not cause soft messy pulps which are hard to separate from the juice. This is especially true of the soft fruit.

Borax, Glycerine of Glycerine of borax is an alternative to bisulphite for use in air locks. It has the advantage that it is not volatilised and driven off by carbon dioxide bubbling through it, as sulphur dioxide is from bisulphite solution.

Bordeaux The area of Western France around the mouth of the Gironde famed for claret. Many of the wines produced are possessors of an Appellation Controlée label, and this imposes limits on the quantity as well as quality of their harvests. The main grape grown is the cabernet. It is high in tannin content and this confers longevity on the wines and means that many of the better wines require 15–20 years before reaching their peak, especially as claret is a dry wine with no residual sugar to mask astringency.

Boring Corks If you are unwise enough not to buy ready-bored corks, it is possible and not too difficult to bore your own. It requires a good eye, for a cork should be bored half way from each side, and, of course, there should be no step in the bore.

Botrytis Cinerea A mould which attacks grapes in warm humid conditions. In the Sauternes region, this disease of vines is encouraged to infect the crop, for if, after infection, there is a dry spell, the mould, in feeding itself, takes water from the grapes, causing them to shrink. The result is a grape with a high sugar content. Similarly, the acidity is raised, but not excessively.

Bottles come in many shapes, sizes and colours, and some wines have their own distinctive type of bottle. These range from the *Methuselah* (a bottle equal to 8 normal bottles of Champagne) to the miniature liqueur bottles, each with its particular shape.

Bottle Brushes A self-descriptive piece of equipment for cleaning bottles! Varying in size, they will cope with air locks or carboys.

Bottle Fermentation Any fermentation taking place in the bottle.

> (a) **Champagne** In order to 'get' the bubbles into the bottle and the wine a second fermentation is required. After the wine has fermented to dryness it is blended, sugar added together with a special champagne yeast, and it is fermented in the bottle.
>
> (b) **Malo-Lactic** If not inhibited by sulphite or too high an alcohol content a wine with a high malic acid content may, if lactobacilli are present, undergo a bottle fermentation whilst converting malic acid to lactic. BUT beware of blown corks.
>
> (c) **Unwanted** will occur if a wine is bottled before fermentation is finished with resulting possibilities of, if lucky, a mess with a blown cork, or, at worst, a burst bottle and a worse mess! Therefore, do not bottle until certain fermentation is finished, despite instructions in some books and recipes to bottle after three days' fermentation.

Bottle, Maturing in Once oxidative changes are far enough advanced, and here experience is the best guide, the air supply to the maturing wine is cut off by bottling. In the bottle, oxidation does still continue, but slowly, while other reactions—reduction reactions—take place. Far more important than these are the esterifications which, over a period of time, result in the wine acquiring a marked bouquet, rounder flavour, and what is known as the marriage of the components.

Bottle Racks are designed for bottles to lie on their side with a small amount of wine in contact with the cork. This prevents drying of the cork which, if it were to occur, would result in shrinkage of the cork and seepage of the wine, with a possibly corked wine. Fortified wines are usually stored upright as alcohol gradually destroys cork. Table wines are safe from this due to their lower alcohol content. (See Suberin).

Bottle Sealing Commercial wine bottles have a lead capsule which effectively protects a wine from acetification should drying of the cork occur. The amateur has a choice of two types of seal—aluminium foil or plastic. The former, while being cheap, probably do not offer such good protection as the latter, which are probably safer for wines intended for long bottle maturing.

Bottle Sickness During bottling it is inevitable that a wine will absorb oxygen and this, unless sulphite is used, will result in the formation of acetaldehyde. The presence of this gives the wine a flat taste and requires at least two or three weeks to disappear.

Bottle Stink Wines sulphited at bottling time often have a marked smell or 'stink' of sulphur dioxide on opening. This is usually only short lived, but may be so strong as to put off completely the prospective drinker. So, sulphite with care at this time; never more than 50 p.p.m.

Bottling The process of transferring the wine from bulk containers to the bottle and sealing it from the air. Like all steps in winemaking, it is to be undertaken with care and strict attention to hygiene.

Bottling Technique The act of transferring wine from one container to another is easy. However, when bottling, care is required to prevent access of oxygen to the wine. Without special equipment involving the use of nitrogen or carbon dioxide this is not possible, but it can be minimised by avoiding splashing and running the wine down the side of the bottle coupled with the use of an anti-oxidant.

Bouquet The term used to cover the description of the smell or aroma of a wine. Under normal conditions this is the result of ester formation from succinic and malic acids joining with alcohol. These esters are fragrant, volatile compounds which, when the wine is slightly warmed, evaporate into the air above the wine, where they should be trapped in the glass so that the bouquet can be enjoyed. If a wine has an unpleasant bouquet infection can be suspected. For optimum ester and, therefore, bouquet development time is the essential factor, although the use of flower petals can confer a pleasing bouquet in a shorter time.

Bouquet, Blending for   See Blending for Bouquet.

Bouquet, Flowers for   Flower petals, especially rose or elderflower, have powerful aromatic bouquet-producing esters which, used in a must at a rate of not more than ½ pint fresh or ¼ oz dried flowers, will have a beneficial effect on the wine. However useful flower esters may be, they do not entirely replace the need for maturing. This is because the marriage of all the congenerics is necessary so that the wine constituents may esterify to produce further esters.

Brandy   is made by distilling wine and, unlike the latter, it only matures in the wood. The best brandy is matured for twenty years or more. During this time the alcohol content falls, due to evaporation losses and also by absorption of atmospheric water. In addition to the aristocratic cognacs and lesser breeds, there is also the cheap *eau de vie de marc*, made from the marc or grape pulp and stalks. This is used for fortification purposes or made into industrial alcohol.

Brass   Due to the copper content brass may cause hazes in wine, as well as discolouration and off flavours. It is therefore safest to make sure that no brass is in contact with wine. Casks with decorative brass hoops are safe, since it is only the collar of the cask that comes into contact with the wine. If contamination does occur it is NOT advised that the amateur attempts curative action, since this involves the use of the highly-toxic potassium ferrocyanide. As copper is toxic it is advised that the wine be discarded should contamination occur. (See Blue Fining).

Breathing   After drawing the cork from red wines, they should (after decanting if required), be allowed to stand for at least an hour without a stopper. During this time oxygen can react with the wine to mellow it prior to drinking.

Brilliance A term used to describe the clarity of a wine which may vary from cloudy to brilliant or star bright (a completely clear wine free from deposit or floating debris).

Brix A scale used instead of specific gravity on the continent. If the degrees Brix are multiplied by 4, the S.G. is obtained approximately. (See Appendix VI).

Brown Sugar is a form of pure sugar containing molasses, hence its colour. It is usually of limited value in wine as it tends to confer a caramel taste and to darken the wine.

Brut A French word to denote extta dryness, usually in a champagne.

Bucket A cheap everyday appliance as useful in winemaking as in the kitchen. The most useful for the winemaker is one of 2 or 5 gallons' capacity with a tight-fitting lid, which is valuable in preparing musts or in conducting pulp fermentation.

Buchner Flask An especially strong flask with an open side arm to take tubing from a vacuum pump to speed filtration by sucking the filtrate through the filter medium.

Buchner Funnel The special funnel with a flat base (as opposed to the normal conical shape). This ensures as large an area as possible is presented to the vacuum to speed filtration.

Budding of Yeast Yeasts are unusual plants in the way that they reproduce. First, a small irregularity appears on the surface of the parent cell. This bud grows until it is a fully formed yeast cell, when it then normally separates from the parent cell.

Buffer Solution is a mixture of a weak acid and its salt, which will tend to minimise a change in pH (by addition of an acid or alkali) by either forming more salt if acid is added, or forming more acid if an alkali is added. A wine is a very complex example of a buffer. It is because of its buffering action that adding a lot of acid to a wine, while increasing the acidity markedly, will only raise the pH slightly. Hence the need, ideally, for measuring both the pH and the acidity of a wine.

Bulk Maturing Wines stored in large containers tend to mature more slowly, which is an ideal situation for quality. It is, however, especially important to choose the size of cask carefully that is to be used for white wines, due to possible oxidation of the wine. The volume of a cask and its surface area are the two factors which determine the rate of entry of air and, if this is too great, the contents will, if left in cask too long, become oxidised. Even with a 9 gallon cask, a white wine will not stand more than 2–3 months in cask, while a red wine may continue to improve for many years.

Bungs are either of plastic or rubber. Whilst economic in that they can be used repeatedly, they are not ideal for maturing purposes, for which cork stoppers only should be used. (The small amount of air that can pass through works wonders on the quality of the wine.) Care must be taken with rubber bungs, for they tend to stick to glass and, if fermentation is still in progress . . . disaster!

Burette An accurately calibrated tube used in titration. There is usually a tap to regulate liquid flow. The burette is filled to the zero mark with alkali which is slowly added to the wine until the end point is reached, when the amount of alkali used is read off from the scale.

Burgundy Yeast One of the many pure strains of yeast available to the amateur. It is particularly suitable for dry wines made from red fruit.

Butyl Alcohol One of the higher alcohols formed in small amounts during fermentation. Like other higher alcohols, it aids flavour and bouquet. In more than trace amounts, it is a powerful inhibitor of yeast.

Butyric Acid is produced by Bacillus butyricus, one of the spoilage organisms, and will cause the wine to smell of rancid butter. Prevention is by hygiene, and the cure, if this form of spoilage occurs, is by disposal of the wine.

B Vitamins Yeasts require Vitamin B for cell growth and, if lacking, may be the cause of a stuck ferment. Although yeasts require some 6 or 7 of the B vitamins, it is usual and sufficient to add only vitamin B_1, 3 mgs per gallon. (See Aneurine Hydrochloride; Calcium Pantothenate).

By-Products of Fermentation are substances produced by the reactions taking place in the must that result in compounds present in the finished wine *other than ethanol*. These include succinic, lactic and acetic acids; glycerine, acetaldehyde, fusel oils and the higher alcohols.

— C —

Cabernet One of the principal grapes grown in France, from different varieties of which are made such wines as clarets and sauternes.

Cadmium See "Plastic, toxic"

Calcium is a metal. In winemaking it is important in lowering the pH of water. Under normal circumstances tap water has sufficient calcium in it for winemaking, except when making sherry. Since sherry must need to be of a lower pH than other wines, calcium has to be added as gypsum. After fermentation has finished most of the calcium present precipitates out of solution as insoluble calcium salts.

Calcium Carbonate is a chemical substance whose use in winemaking is one of the standard methods of reducing acidity. The addition of $\frac{1}{4}$ oz (7 gms) per gallon will lower the acidity by about 1·5 ppt of sulphuric acid. The reaction involves the formation of insoluble calcium salts and the giving off of carbon dioxide. So beware of foaming.

Calcium Pantothenate is one of the B group of vitamins and is present in nearly all winemaking ingredients. Rarely it may be deficient to such an extent as to cause a stuck ferment.

However, as there is usually enough present in the must and starter to prevent this, it is not considered essential as an additive. Its action is that of an enzyme in the reaction which oxidises pyruvic acid to acetaldehyde.

Calcium Sulphate See Gypsum.

Calibrated Jars are useful pieces of equipment for measuring fruit juices at pressing time. Measurement is important both with regard to yield of juice and also for working out necessary dilutions to achieve the proper balance in the must.

Campden Tablets contain about 450 mg of potassium or sodium metabisulphite. These are added crushed and are used as sterilising agents. The usual rate is two tablets per gallon for sterilising the must; the same at the first racking; and one tablet at successive rackings. The actions of metabisulphite are dealt with under Sulphite and Sterilising.

Candida A genus of yeasts called imperfecta due to the fact that they are incapable of forming spores. There are many species, varying from those which cause Thrush in man to wine spoilage organisms.

Candida Albicans The type species of Candida (it is the main species and all others are identified by reference to it). This is the species responsible for the condition known as Thrush; it is, however, not a wine spoilage organism.

Candida Mycoderma The species of Candida of greatest importance to the winemaker. It is a film yeast and is most commonly seen as a greyish-green scum or skin on the surface of the lees in the bottom of unwashed bottles. It is an aerobic organism and forms a pellicle or skin on the surface of the wine. At the same time it converts the alcohol to carbon dioxide and water. Infection starts as small whitish patches on the surface of the wine which gradually increase in size and join together to form the pellicle. Prevention is by hygiene and anaerobic conditions. Cure is to sulphite the wine heavily and break up the pellicle. After a few days, the particles sink to the bottom of the container and the wine can be racked off.

Candy Sugar is an expensive way of buying pure sugar, since granulated sugar is also pure. Many recipes recommend its use because they were drawn up in the days of grades of purity of sugar and they have not been updated. Some people claim it confers a better flavour on the wine; which, like many things, is a matter of personal preference.

Cane Sugar is refined from the juice of the sugar cane. Until recent years it was the only source of pure sugar, but with the improvement in refining techniques for beet sugar it forms only about two-thirds of sugar consumed in the U.K. As long as the packet says it contains *pure sugar*, it does not matter what name it goes by or its parentage, since its effect on the wine is the same whether the sugar is derived from cane or beet.

Canned Fruit A most useful and restful way of picking fruit! Provided care is exercised in the choice, there is no reason why good wines cannot be made. However, for dry wines it is essential to ensure that no artificial sweetening agents have been used, for some of these are non-fermentable and, despite no residual sugar on assay, the wine will be sweet to the taste.

Cap, Crown The name given to the metal caps used for sealing bottles. Mostly used for beer, they have in recent years come to be used for the second stage of champagne making (bottle fermentation). They have the advantage over cork of cost and of course the wine cannot become corked. They require a special tool for their application, but are much easier than champagne corks both to fit and remove!

Cap of Pulp At the start of a pulp fermentation the pulped fruit lies at the bottom of the fermentation vessel but, within a few days, as carbon dioxide production increases, the gas entrapped between particles of fruit raises these to the surface to form the Cap of Pulp. It is at this stage that infection is most likely to occur and, to prevent this, in addition to ensuring maximum extraction from the pulp, the cap should be broken up twice a day and the must roused. It is useful to use a sinker to hold the cap below the surface.

Capsules Theoretically, these are used to seal the wine and its cork from the air, to prevent the wine from becoming corked. However, some capsules have holes pierced in them which destroys this hypothesis. Whether the pierced ones were originally intended for bottles expected to take years to come to maturity and therefore might benefit from some air is not certain. However, it is certain that they are decorative, thereby increasing the appeal of the wine.

Capsules, Alloy are a method of decorating bottles and also protecting the cork from spoilage. They are available in a wide variety of colours and, although not providing the best cork protection for long storage, they are certainly the cheapest.

Capsules, Lead Most commercial wines have lead capsules on them. When opening a bottle protected in this way it is important to remove the whole capsule and not merely the top half-inch or so. This is because lead is a toxic metal which will not gain entry to the wine when used as a seal but, if not removed, may contaminate it. As lead is an accumulative poison its effects are not immediately seen.

Capsules, Plastic The amateur's "posh" capsule. Available in various colours, they are shrink fitted and will, as well as enhancing the look of the bottle, protect it from possible corking. There are two types available—one is kept moist and pliable in a special solution and, after placing on the bottle, shrinks to the shape of the bottle as it dries; the other comes as a rigid cylinder and requires softening before use. Both are equally effective but the latter is more finished in looks as it will not shrink unevenly, as may the former.

Caramel When sugar is heated above its melting point it turns from white to brown as it loses its structure and becomes amorphous. This brown substance is called caramel and is used for colouring and flavouring wines, particularly the dessert and sweet types. Delicate table wines should not have caramel added for its powerful aroma and taste will obscure the intended flavour.

Caramelisation The term used to describe the taste of

madeira-like wines which, due to the heating processes involved in their manufacture, develop a burnt sugar (or caramel) taste.

Carbohydrate Organic compounds composed of carbon, hydrogen and oxygen; from which elements is derived the name. For winemakers, the carbohydrates of importance are the sugars.

Carbon Used in its pure form—charcoal—it is a useful fining agent for either lightening an over-dark wine or for removing taints. It is a substance which requires very careful trial finings before scale use, since over-use will result in a colourless, flavourless wine. It is used to this end in the manufacture of Vodka.

Carbon Cycle All organic material in nature circulates from the earth to animals and/or man and back to the soil. Carbon is only slightly different in that it is also present in the atmosphere as carbon dioxide and is utilised for plant photosynthesis. This recycling of carbon is the carbon cycle, and winemaking plays its part in the release of carbon dioxide from sugar while producing alcohol. (See Appendix IX).

Carbon Dioxide is nature's waste product. In almost all chemical reactions in nature resulting in waste it is carbon dioxide which is that product. This holds true for winemaking where the conversion of sugar to alcohol results in an equal weight of carbon dioxide being given off. This is, unless a sparkling wine is being produced, a waste product, although it helps protect against infection. (See Appendix IX).

Carbonates These are salts present in tap water and contribute to its pH and hardness. Since carbonates precipitate on boiling care must be taken with pH analysis if boiled water is to be used as there is the possibility that the pH may be increased with its use and the bacterial protection afforded by a low pH will be lost.

Carbonation is achieved by forcing carbon dioxide into a bottle under pressure (a dangerous technique for the amateur), or by encouraging a bottle fermentation as in champagne making or as seen in the case of a malo-lactic fermentation. In commercial "fizzy" drinks, a pressure of 90 psi is not uncommon, but this is dangerously high for the amateur who ought not to aim for more than 50 psi.

Carbonic Acid Carbon dioxide is very soluble in water and when it enters solution it partially dissociates and forms a weak acid. This acid is carbonic acid. It plays an important part in the buffering of fermenting wines, but when fermentation is complete and the carbon dioxide is lost, obviously so too is the carbonic acid. When racking a young wine the presence of carbonic acid helps to prevent oxidation by reacting with the oxygen absorbed.

Carbonyl Chemical compounds chiefly responsible for the bouquet of a wine. They are all members of the aldehyde or ketone series.

Carboxylase One of the most important enzymes in alcohol production. It is secreted by yeasts and its action is to promote the decarboxylation (removal of carbon) of pyruvic acid to acetaldehyde. In the process carbon dioxide is given off. Unlike most of the reactions involved in alcohol production this one is irreversible.

Carboys Large glass containers usually of 5 or 10 gallon capacity ideally suited to the larger scale producer.

Casein The principal protein of milk. In its pure form (although expensive), it is an excellent fining agent. It is superior to charcoal as a decolouring agent since it does not absorb flavours. The best way of using it is to dissolve the casein either in strong ammonia and then boil until the ammonia is driven off, or to dissolve it in sodium bicarbonate. It is common to prepare a tannin-casein mixture of equal proportion for fining, as tannin will combine with any excess protein to aid clearing. (See Copper).

Cask Another term for wooden storage vessels for wine. There is no doubt that oak casks are the best containers for a quality wine but unfortunately their high cost precludes their routine use. Even in France their use is dying out since, sad to say, there are no longer any craftsmen who can make, maintain or repair those beautiful fermentation vats so often seen in pictures. Instead, with modern progress, the use of concrete and glass, or plastic, has taken the place of wood.

Cask Care More than any piece of equipment do casks require close attention. The wood of a cask left empty for any time will shrink with the result that the hoops and staves will become loose. Casks not cleaned immediately after use will rapidly acquire taints difficult to eradicate. Thus, the cardinal rule of using casks is to ensure cleanliness and always to refill the cask within an hour or two of emptying it. If not refilling it with wine, it should be partially filled with sterilising solution.

Cask Cleaning Immediately after emptying, a cask must be cleaned out, otherwise it may become tainted. All that is required are general washes with tap water to ensure that all sediment has been removed. The cask can then be sterilised for re-use.

Cask, Half A cask sawn in half is a romantic container to crush fruit in, especially grapes. However, the difficulty of cleaning such a piece of equipment allied to its high cost makes it a démodé crushing vat. For the modern winemaker the prosaic dustbin is better.

Cask Maturing is accepted as being the best method of maturing wine. Any winemaker concerned with quality production is well advised to have at least one barrel for just this purpose. Maturing in cask firstly fulfils the axiom that bulk maturing is better than maturing in small volumes. Secondly, the wood has pores in it large enough to allow the passage of air while excluding bacteria. The size of these pores is such that a continuous stream of air can reach the wine at a rate which will ensure an optimum rate of oxidative changes. This is obviously preferable to the wine receiving massive doses of air at racking, with concomitant chances of over-oxidation. Thirdly, the wood and wine exchange substances to the ultimate effect of the wine. (See Maturation.)

Cask, Oxidation in Since wood has pores through which air can enter the wine, a wine matured in the wood will always be receiving some oxygen to allow oxidative changes to take place. The rate of reaction depends on the ratio of air entering the wine to the volume of the wine. Thus in a large cask the air supply may be insufficient so that regular rackings are required to augment the oxygen reaching the wine. This problem is unlikely to be met with in amateur cask sizes, since they are usually less than 9 gallons. If anything, the opposite is more likely to occur, since the small casks used mean a large surface/volume ratio, so that the wine is in fact in danger of over-oxidation. To prevent this careful judgement is needed to gauge the optimum length of cask maturing. Once a wine is clear, it should not be racked (this may cause over-oxidation) unless removing the wine from a deposit. White wines are less robust than reds and cannot withstand long periods of cask maturing. Depending on the tannin content of a red wine, it may be capable of withstanding several years' cask maturing; a white wine, on the other hand, will spoil and become over-oxidised after only a few months. For sherry-type wines, prolonged oxidation is a required feature of their production.

Cask, Preparation for use After ensuring that the hoops are tight, a new barrel requires the staves to be swollen by filling it for 24–48 hours with water. This is followed by hot soda washes until the water comes out clear. The soda is then rinsed out with tap water. After sterilising with bisulphite, 5 gms per gallon, the barrel is ready for use.

Cask Sizes The most popular barrel sizes for the amateur are the $4\frac{1}{2}$ and 6 gallon casks, and these, with careful regulation of the time a wine is allowed to remain in the wood, suffice for most people. The range of sizes is from 3 to 54 gallons, and there should be one among these to suit everybody!

Cask Size, Choice of For the amateur, space, manageability and scale of production will dictate the size. For most, sizes above 9 gallons are too unwieldy. Usually 3, $4\frac{1}{2}$ or 6 gallons are the sizes of choice. With such cooperage there is no difficulty in must preparation, racking (don't forget 18 gallons of wine require 36 gallons cooperage), or handling of full casks.

Casks, Sterilisation of   The old method of burning sulphur wicks inside the barrel has been superseded by the use of sulphite, since burning sulphur tends to drip, and these may confer a 'bad egg' flavour to the wine. The 5 per cent stock sulphite solution is quite adequate.

Cask Storage   *Never keep a cask on its side without proper supports.* They should always be kept on their sides but supported at each end in order to prevent warping, and should have stillages to prevent rolling about, as well as bearing at least part of the weight. If being kept empty, a cask should have a few pints of stock sulphite in it and the cask upended. It should be turned every few weeks to ensure total sterility.

Cask Topping up   Due to the pores in the wood, there is an inevitable loss of water and alcohol to the atmosphere. It is essential to prevent the over-oxidation which will occur should the cask become too empty, and therefore the casks must be topped up at regular intervals with a wine of a similar type to that maturing. (See Topping up)

Cask, Ullage   Due to the loss of contents by evaporation, an air-space develops above the wine in a cask, which is known as ullage.

Casse   A discolouration of a wine due to enzyme or metallic contamination.

Casse, Metallic   Copper, lead, tin and iron will, if allowed contact with a wine, cause a haze and discolouration in the wine, which will also have a marked metallic taste. If lead is suspected as the contaminant, the wine must be discarded, since lead is highly toxic. This usually affects wine as the result of using old earthenware vessels with a soft glaze. It is sometimes possible to remove an iron haze by the use of bentonite and tannin finings. Prevention of any metallic casse is by avoiding the use of metal containers except those known to be safe.

Casse, Oxidative   Wines made from over-ripe fruit, especially pears and apples, contain large amounts of an enzyme called o-polyphenoloxidase which has the action of oxidising tannins to brown pigments; hence the discolouration. Prevention is by immediate sulphiting of prepared fruit. Cure is by sulphiting the wine with 50–100 ppt sulphite every 2–3 months until the problem is overcome (an instance of sulphite being used as an anti-oxidant). The sulphite will take up the oxygen before the enzyme, and so prevent the fault developing further.

Casse, Oxidassic Another term for oxidative casse.

Castor Sugar The fine form of sugar used for sprinkling over fruit etc. This dissolves more easily than granulated sugar but does not confer any superiority on a wine compared with other forms of pure sugar.

Catalyst Some chemical reactions progress so slowly that without help from other compounds they would make almost none of the final compound. Chemicals which speed up these reactions are called catalysts. They act by forming intermediate products, which are then changed into the final compound. The most peculiar characteristic of catalysts is that they are not changed at the end of the reaction that they catalyse. Thus, a small amount of a catalyst can speed up a large amount of compounds reacting together. Reactions needing catalysts are speeded up by increasing the temperature, but if it is raised too much the reaction will slow down since catalysts are often denatured by heat as other proteins.

Catechol A tannin of simple structure present in the grape, which contributes most of the astringency to a finished wine.

Cellar With high rise flats it is hard to see anyone running down 25 flights of stairs to fetch a bottle of wine from the cellar! Unfortunately, all too often existing cellars tend to be damp (a perfect environment for moulds). But where there is a dry cellar it is the ideal place for a wine store, since the temperature can be kept constant while the sun is excluded. Nowadays the 'cupboard under the stairs' has to double as a coat store and a wine cellar!

Cellarcraft embraces the care of wine from the moment a must finishes fermenting until it is served at table. This involves maturing, bottling, corking, labelling, storage and, finally, serving the wine.

Cellulose is the main building block in the plant kingdom, akin to protein in animals. It is composed of long chains of glucose. Enzymes capable of breaking it down are rare—mostly they are secreted by putrefactive bacteria, such as those which cause the sweet smell of decaying grass. However, there is now available to the amateur an enzymatic preparation—Rohament P—which is able to break down connective tissue in plants (this is composed chiefly of cellulose). By breaking down the plant to this extent, the yield of juice is increased.

Cellulose and Filtration Cellulose is now becoming a valuable filtering agent to the winemaker, taking the place of asbestos. (See Filtration and Cellulose.)

Cépage A term used in Alsace for grading the grapes; perhaps the most easily understood translation, though not entirely accurate, is quality. Its actual meaning is the vines themselves.

Cereal See Grain

Chalk See Calcium carbonate.

Chalk, Reducing Acidity with See Acid reduction; Calcium carbonate.

Champagne *The* sparkling wine. Credits for its development are given to the monk, Dom Perignon, who 'invented' Champagne corks to preserve the 'fizz', and to the Widow Cliquot, who invented the pupitre and rémuage. Most likely, its development is related to the drinking of wines much younger than now, to minimise the chances of acetification, and the discovery that carbon dioxide (present in any wine still fermenting when bottled) masked some of the faults of older wines.

Champagne Bottles Because of the pressures encountered in commercial Champagne the bottles are thicker and heavier than ordinary wine bottles. It cannot be stressed strongly enough that champagne-type wines must not be put into weak wine or damaged sparkling wine bottles—'else the wine runneth out'. Always check bottles for flaws whether scratches or chips; if present, discard that bottle. *If in doubt about a sparkling wine bottle, do not use it.*

Champagne Bottles, Pressure in Commercially, this is between 70 and 90 pounds per square inch (psi). But, for amateur winemakers, it is recommended that the pressure should not exceed 50 psi. Firstly, there is a danger in working with these wines, particularly when disgorging, and secondly, the bottles may have flaws unsuspected by the winemaker. With common sense and care, however, the chances of danger are very small. (See Champagne, Sugar Additions).

Champagne Making consists of several special steps after fermenting and blending the dry base wine. The wine is sweetened and re-fermented in the bottle and, when this is complete, the sediment is collected in the neck by inverting the bottle over a period of time (rémuage), and finally the loss of wine from disgorging is made good. The wine is then matured and sold.

Champagne, Sugar Additions prior to re-fermentation must be carefully gauged to obtain the maximum sparkle consistent with safety. The recommended amounts are given in Appendix VIII.

Champagne Yeast A pure strain of yeast which is unusual in that it can ferment in the presence of a high concentration of carbon dioxide. For successful sparkling winemaking this yeast is essential, especially for the bottle fermentation.

Chaptalisation The addition of sugar to commercial musts in a poor year when the natural sugar of the grape is not sufficient to yield a high enough alcohol level. The amount permitted is regulated by law in France and the process takes its name from its inventor, M. Chaptal. In virtually all amateur winemaking this is a normal practice, as it is rare to find a fruit high enough in sugar to give a satisfactory wine, except for the wine grape.

Charcoal is one of the purest forms of carbon. It is very active chemically and can combine with most dyes and esters so that, if used for fining, care must be taken not to use too much in case a white, tasteless liquid is all that is left.

Charmat Process A method of making sparkling wines frowned upon by the Champenois. It entails the second fermentation taking place in a sealed tank. (See Cuvée close.)

Chateau In the Bordeaux region of France many of the vineyards have the title 'Chateau' conferred upon them as a mark of consistent high quality wine production. Although the word means *Castle*, it is used in much the same sense as we use the term 'Estate'.

Chemical Extraction of Flavour See Extraction, Chemical

Chlorine has two actions to the winemaker; one beneficial, the other annoying. On the good side, it is in the form of bleach, a powerful cleaning and sterilising agent. It is, on the other hand, an inhibitor of yeast, should the water supply have too high a concentration. This problem can be overcome by the use of bisulphite, 50 ppm, before innoculation with yeast.

Chlorophyl The green pigment present in leaves responsible for plant respiration. Yeasts are unusual plants in that they do not contain this compound and therefore cannot utilise sunlight to obtain energy as do all other plants. Instead, we utilise *them* to make alcohol!

Cider A weakly alcoholic drink made from the fermented juice of apples. Unlike the must prepared for apple wine production the cider must is high in tannin. The use of bitter apples is responsible for this freshness and bite to be found in a good cider.

Citral An example of a bouquet producing compound which is an aldehyde.

Citric Acid Until the recent advent on the winemaking scene of cheap supplies of other acids, citric acid was the winemaker's staple. Its main use is that it aids a healthy ferment and also has good antiseptic properties. For maturing purposes it is almost useless since it is not utilised in ester formation. Thus it is not recommended for use on its own. However, for the beginner not wishing to delve into the mysteries of the other acids its use in the correct amounts is not to be sneered at. It will give a pleasant acid character to a wine and after all lemonade has long been an introduction to 'hard drinking'!

Citrus Peel and Inhibition Do not allow the pith of citrus fruit into the must. It contains an oil which forms a layer on the surface of the must, thus preventing oxygen access to aid establishment of a fermenting yeast colony.

Clarification The stage of wine production that immediately follows fermentation when, by gravitational and electrical forces, the cloudiness of a wine gradually lessens until a starbright wine is seen. On occasions, luckily rare, the wine refuses to clear on its own and other methods have to be resorted to, to obtain a clear wine. To avoid the need for fining requires the use of the proper enzymes at the start of fermentation. If, despite their use, a cloudy wine remains, fining and filtering are then indicated.

Clarification and Pectin Most members of the plant kingdom contain pectin in varying quantities and if, in a wine, pectin is not broken down, the result will be a haze, due to its entering colloidal solution. To obviate this possibility the routine use of pectin destroying enzymes prior to fermentation is recommended; especially in the case of pulp fermentation, to aid extraction of juice, colour and aromatic compounds.

Clarification and Refrigeration Many substances causing hazes are only partially soluble and by lowering the temperature they are forced out of solution, precipitate and leave a clear wine. A good example of this is tartaric acid and its potassium salts. It is important to rack the wine at as near the refrigeration temperature as possible in order to prevent these substances re-entering solution. The old practice of racking a wine after a few days' frost was a simple means of practicing this technique before the advent of modern technology.

Clarification and Sulphite Apart from inhibiting the growth of a new yeast colony from the remaining cells after racking, sulphite also aids clearing by neutralising the electrical charges on some colloidal particles so that they precipitate out of suspension.

Clarification and Tannin Tannin has the ability to combine with protein to form insoluble coagulates. Thus any suspected and diagnosed protein haze requires treatment with tannin after trial finings.

Clarity The term used to describe the clearness, or limpidity, of a wine. If there are no hazes, foreign bodies or deposits, and the wine is absolutely translucent, then it is described as being 'star bright'. The descendant stages are: clear, hazy and cloudy. The last term being used for a wine which is obviously opaque.

Classification of Sugars Sugars are classified by the number of carbon atoms in their basic sugar unit (ie *a hexose* has 6 carbon units), and by the number of units of basic sugar that comprise one molecule of the sugar. For example, *glucose* is a hexose monosaccharide (it has a single unit of six carbons in its molecule). On the other hand, *sucrose* is a hexose disaccharide, since it has two units of six carbons in its structure.

Classification of Wines Wines are classified according to *type;* aperitif, social, table or dessert; *colour;* red, white, rosé, brown or golden; and *sweetness;* dry, medium or sweet.

Cleaning The first step to the production of sound wines is scrupulous cleanliness in everything which includes oneself as well as all the equipment one uses!

Cleaning Agents See bacteria; Bleach; boiling; sterilising; sulphite.

Cleaning Casks See Casks, care Casks, cleaning.

Cleaning Equipment See Sterilizing entries.

Clearing The term used to describe the falling out from suspension of yeast débris and other sediments in the wine. Some of this occurs by gravity, ie fruit pulp and yeast; some by coagulation, ie protein-tannin complexes; and other compounds may have to be persuaded out of solution by various means, such as fining and filtering.

Clinitest A test reagent in tablet form which measures the concentration of glucose in the wine. It is essential in the making of sparkling wines to know the residual sugar before dosage. The method of use is described under Sugar Estimation in Wine. (See Quantan RC).

Clostridium Species of bacteria, one of which causes tetanus or lockjaw. These bacteria are especially resistant to many of the sterilising agents because, as spore forming bacteria, they can defend themselves from many of the bacteriocidal agents. They are only killed by very high temperatures maintained for long periods. They are, however, prevented from reproducing if the pH is below 4·5. Thus, to ensure a must or equipment free from these bacteria, it is necessary to assay the pH, since the practicality of 'autoclaving' equipment is beyond the amateur. Of course, it would destroy the wine to heat it or its ingredients for any length of time.

Closures, Plastic Useful re-usable 'corks' which are usually flanged. They vary from almost flat such as are used with crown caps, to bottle and champagne types. Although moderately expensive to buy they can with care be re-used many times. It is most important to ensure that they are of a good fit to prevent seepage.

Cloth, Pressing Muslin or terylene cloth of a fine weave which is used to wrap fruit before placing it in the press. If no cloth is used great difficulty may be experienced in cleaning the press after use as the pulp will be forced into the cracks and drainage holes.

Cloth, Straining Any fine weave cloth containing no dyes or starch is ideal. Its purpose is to restrain particles of fruit pulp from entering the fermentation vessel after pressing the fruit.

Cloudiness The term used to describe a wine which has an obvious degree of opacity, usually when the opposite side of the container is not clearly visible. (See Diagnosis of Faults, Appendix XI).

Coagulation A phenomenon which occurs at the iso-electric point of a protein. Proteins are peculiar in that they can form either acids or bases depending on the pH of their solution. However, at the iso-electric point, they can form neither and lose their colloidal state, and fall out of solution or coagulate. Thus any change in the pH of a wine will increase the chances of protein coagulation. This is likely to happen if two wines are blended. To prevent this occurring after bottling, blended wines must be allowed to stand a few months.

Cod-Liver Oil is rich in B vitamins, (which is the reason for Mrs. Squeers' predilection for it at Dotheboys Hall). It is not recommended for wine-makers, since the unmistakable, and horrible, flavour and bouquet will be conferred on the wine with resulting disapproval from drinkers! So, do not buy malt extracts, unless free from this bodybuilding substance!

Co-Enzymes are molecules usually smaller than their specific enzymes and are essential for its action. Often they act as carriers of ions from the substrate being acted on to an appropriate acceptor. Co-enzyme I accepts hydrogen ions from pyruvic acid to become dihydrocoenzyme I which, in order to fulfil the maxim that enzymes are not used up, is then changed back to its original structure. Having accepted hydrogen from a molecule of pyruvic acid, the specific enzyme zymase can then perform its part in oxidising acetaldehyde to alcohol.

Co-Factor These have the same function as co-enzymes, but they are usually metals in their various ionic forms, instead of being complex organic molecules.

Co-Ferment Another term for co-enzyme.

Coffee Spoon See Appendix XII.

Colander A useful piece of equipment for straining musts It can usually be borrowed from the kitchen, so long as it is made of plastic.

Cold Extraction To minimise pectin extraction, and prevent undue destruction of volatile oils the use of cold water and pectic enzyme is advised for most ingredients. The method is to place the crushed fruit in a volume of cold water about equal to half the final volume of must. Sulphite is added both to sterilise the fruit and to neutralise excess chlorine in the water. To aid extraction, pectin and cellulose destroying enzymes are added. If desired, pulp fermentation can then follow. The type of fruit to which this method is suited are: apples, citrus fruit, peaches, pears, and rhubarb.

Collage A French word meaning *fining*.

Collagen An animal protein (it is found in man too, where it is a connective tissue), which when boiled is altered to gelatin—a fining agent.

Collagenous Protein Any protein which can be degraded to gelatin by heating.

Colloids Some substances, when placed in a liquid, are not soluble and, instead of falling to the bottom of the container, as would, say, chalk, remain floating. For this to happen, the substance must be finely ground with a particle size between one-thousandth and one-millionth of a centimetre. The particles (or dispersed phase) have an electrical charge, which acts like similar poles of a magnet and repel each other. Because of this effect, the particles remain in colloidal suspension and form a haze. Protein is the common cause of such a fault. In winemaking, the main colloidal fining agent is Bentonite, which forms a lyophobic colloid (the wine and bentonite do not have an affinity for each other and will not combine together chemically). If there is protein present, the negatively charged bentonite will be attracted to the positively charged protein. They will form electrically neutral particles which, as well as being too large to remain in suspension, no longer have the repelling charges, and fall out of suspension to produce a clear wine.

Colour Extraction Obtaining the correct depth of colour in a must is one of the most important steps in the production of wines. For white wines, the only required action is the use of the right quantities of ingredients. For red wines it is usual to ferment initially on the fruit pulp before straining the must after the necessary depth of colour has been achieved. Rosé wines, being light red wine, need less pulp fermentation. The usual length of time required for red wines is between 5 and 7 days; and for rosés, between a few hours and 2 days, depending on the depth of colour required.

Colour of Wine is normally limited to white, rosé or red. Some dessert wines may be golden or brown in colour; as may be sherries. White and rosé are fairly obvious colours, but red has a wide range of shades, all of which are correct within the meaning of the term. Some poor quality reds may be similar in colour to a blackcurrant juice, while a newly made claret may be so dark as to appear almost black (a shade often likened to mahogany). This colour fades gradually to a shade sometimes called brick red. An orange colour in a wine may be due to a failed attempt to blend a red wine and a white wine to obtain a rosé; green is not an uncommon shade in a young white wine and is due to the presence of chlorophyll. A brown colour in a white table wine is often due to oxidation. (See Diagnosis of Faults Appendix XI).

Colour, Wrong (See Actinic Action of Sunlight; Diagnosis of Faults, Appendix XI).

Colouring The colour of a wine depends on the amount of fruit, and its colour, used in the preparation of that wine. If it is discovered that a wine is not the correct colour, and blending is not a practical solution, there are a variety of colouring agents available to try to obtain the correct tone. Should a wine be too intense in colour, then blending with a neutral topping-up type of wine will possibly overcome the problem. It is rare for a red wine to be too dark in colour.

Colouring, Natural Agents Red or brown pigments are derived from tannins; yellow or green from chlorophyll; red, purple and blue from anthocyanins; yellow from anthoxanthins. At least one of these pigments is present in all living plant tissue. Those that are insoluble in water will require alcoholic leaching (or dissolving), achieved by pulp fermentation. It is fascinating to think that these pigments are all composed of the same elements in different arrangements and that, by altering one single atom, a different colour can be produced.

Commercial Imitations Many amateur winemakers, not content with making a country wine, try to emulate commercial products. This can, with care and attention to details of ingredient blending, be achieved. By careful analysis of the taste and characteristics of a wine, it is possible to blend ingredients to simulate, with a passable success, a chosen commercial type.

Competitions are now a frequent occurrence in the winemaker's diary. Apart from prizewinning, there is always plenty to learn from the judges' comments, and this should bring about an improvement in one's standards. When entering a competition, be careful to study the rules and obey them, otherwise that prizewinning wine will be eliminated, maybe because there was only a small rule broken, such as the wrong amount of air space.

Composition of Wines Obviously, the composition of a wine depends to a large extent on its ingredients. However, there are many compounds common to all wines: see Acid; Aldehyde; Carbon Dioxide; Ester; Glycerol; Ketone; Pectin; Protein; Salts; Sugar; Sulphur; Tannin; and Water.

Concentrate, Grape One of the major advances in food technology is the ability to condense and sterilise a juice to a S.G. of maybe 400 without losing any of the volatile aromatic constituents. There are many firms now marketing grape concentrates, from which can be made excellent wines. The basic method of concentrating a juice and, at the same time, retaining the flavour, is by using the technique known as vacuum evaporation. This entails, as the term implies, the lowering of the pressure in the boiling container so that the boiling point of the juice is also lowered. By boiling at a lower temperature, less of the volatile oils are driven off, since the temperature can be lowered below their boiling point.

Conditioning Casks See Casks, Preparation for use.

Congeneric These are the higher alcohols and esters present in a wine or spirit responsible for conferring bouquet and flavour on the drink. In distilling spirits the congenerics can be altered by changing the technique of distillation.

Containers Any winemaking utensil, usually closable either by its lid or with a bung or airlock, used for fermentating or maturing wines. Any non-reactive material is safe.

Containers, Earthenware Until recently, the traditional amateur winemaking fermenter. However, due to rising costs, the fact that one is unable to see what is happening within and, far more important, the danger of using a jar glazed with lead based glazes, they are going out of use to a great extent. These are toxic since the lead will be leached into the wine.

Containers, Enamel Provided the enamel is not chipped, these are safe. Once chipped the metal comes into contact with the wine causing hazes, due to the iron which forms the basic jar.

Containers, Glass These are undoubtedly the best. They are easy to clean, and since they are transparent it is possible to inspect the contents. Due to the ease of cleaning, they are equally easy to sterilise and, most important, they are to all intents non-reactive. Thus no ingredients can attack the glass and destroy it or cause off-flavours—not all plastics are safe from this. Do not keep wine in clear glass containers in direct sunlight. (See Actinic Action of Sunlight)

Containers, Glazing of Many old earthenware containers are glazed using a lead-based glaze, which can be recognised by its softness. The salt-based glazes are safe from toxic effects, and these do not indent with pressure. Lead is a toxic metal and should not be allowed into contact with wine.

Containers, Oak See Casks.

Containers, Plastic Provided the plastic is of a 'food grade', that is to say of a tough plastic, it is quite safe to use for fermentation, since it is guaranteed non-toxic. Recently, the scare about cadmium used to colour some yellow containers has been laid to rest.

Containers, Stoneware Synonymous with Earthenware.

Continuous Filters usually work on the syphon principle to take hazy wine to the filters, which can be based on cellulose, asbestos or on epoxy bonded silicates. Apart from asbestos, they are non-toxic. Provided the filter does not become blocked, the whole volume of wine to be cleared can be left to its own devices, unlike using filter paper and funnel, which require topping up, In addition, as long as instructions are followed, there is little likelihood of over-oxidation occurring.

'Cooking' Fruit Although in the final analysis personal choice dictates ingredients and the choice of variety used, many people consider that the kitchen varieties are the best for winemaking. This no doubt arises from the fact that these varieties contain a higher acid level than their dessert counterparts. However, with the availability of acids today, there is no reason why any non-poisonous species should not contribute to a wine.

Cooperage The art of making and repairing wooden barrels. It is interesting to note that in the 16th century it meant the sampling and bottling of wines.

Copper if present in a wine, is usually in the form of cupric sulphide. This soluble salt causes discolouration and off-flavour in the wine. A wine which has a reddish haze or deposit must be suspected of having a copper contamination. The best method of removal is by use of the dangerous ferrocyanide, which is not for the amateur. However, the use of casein may reduce the level sufficiently to render the wine drinkable.

Cordial A non-alcoholic beverage usually prepared from fruit juices and then sweetened; sometimes to excess for the adult palate.

Cork is obtained from the outer bark of the cork oak. It is only since the discovery of cork that vintage wines have become commonplace. Cork properly cut has good sealant properties, while allowing small volumes of air to gain entry to the wine to aid maturing. The natural 'glue' holding cork together—suberin—is slightly soluble in alcohol. If in contact long enough the cork may be dissolved. With table wines this is not likely to occur, but fortified wines with their higher alcohol content are usually stored upright to prevent this. Port is the exception to this rule, since the wax over the cork acts as a further safeguard.

Cork, Champagne These are made in three parts and glued together. They differ from the normal straight cork in that they are much wider at the base than the apex. Many modern Champagnes are now being stoppered with plastic closures.

Cork, Flanged These are not recommended for table wines intended for laying down. They are shorter than the standard cork and also, having a slight taper, are more liable to leakage if laid on their sides. They are, however, ideal for aperitifs, where the bottle is opened more than once (maybe!). They are also obligatory for competitions held under the rules laid down by the Amateur Winemakers National Guild of Judges.

Cork Injuries Champagne bottles opened without great care, particularly when emulating successful sportsmen, can travel at speeds of up to 60 mph. This is more than enough to cause the several cases of blindness which occur each year, largely due to negligence.

Cork, Straight Standard These are the corks of choice for any wine destined for maturing. Being of a greater diameter than flanged corks, they are less liable to seepage and spoilage.

Cork, Tapered These corks do not have their full length in contact with the neck of the bottle and are, therefore, not recommended for wine stoppering since leakage can easily occur. They are, however, useful for stock solutions, when a protrusion of the cork is useful for ease of removal.

Cork Wiring All sparkling wines after bottling in champagne bottles and sealing with champagne type corks *must* be wired, to prevent the corks blowing out due to the great pressures exerted on them by the carbon dioxide. Make sure the wire lies in the grooves on the cork.

Corked Wine is one which acquires the smell of a musty cork, due to infection in the cork. This has been variously described as a 'swimming bath smell', or likened to the smell an empty medicine bottle acquires. The condition arises due to infection of the cork causing infection of the wine. This is usually due to shrinkage of the cork, although it may be due to non-sterilisation of corks prior to their insertion.

Corking Equipment varies from the simple 'flogger' to elaborate and expensive professional equipment. For most amateurs, the plastic or wooden hand corkers, which work on the plunger principle, are quite adequate.

Corkscrews The wine drinker's life-preserver!

Cotton Wool A plug of cotton wool used to close a fermentation jar will prevent access of bacteria while permitting free access of air. This is of value during the lag phase of fermentation to encourage a vigourous primary ferment, but if used during the secondary fermentation, it may cause over-oxidation. In sherry production, its use will prevent infection while ensuring the oxidation that is the feature of such wines.

Country Wines are wines made from a single unblended fruit, vegetable or leaf, with the addition of sugar and nutrients only. Nowadays, most amateur winemakers do not make true country wines, since they nearly all blend their ingredients and also add grape juice. As well as this, most winemakers use the proprietory yeasts and not bakers' yeast, which was the staple of the old style winemaker.

Cradles for Casks The specially shaped wooden rests upon which barrels should always be placed. As the cradle is designed to fit the curves of the barrel it will not cause strain on the staves and so prevent warping or springing.

Cream of Tartar The salt of tartaric acid, which has one potassium atom attached to it in place of one of the hydrogen atoms. Thus its chemical name is *monopotassium tartrate*. If present in a wine, it will precipitate out as crystals called *argols*.

Criadera The butts or casks into which a young sherry is placed to undergo initial maturation before passing through the solera. Its literal meaning is nursery.

Crock Any earthenware container.

Crown Caps Commonly used to seal beer bottles, they have recently entered service in Champagne making where they are used to seal the bottles during the bottle fermentation.

Cru A term used to describe the class to which a particular Bordeaux wine belongs. It is derived from the verb *crure*, which means *to grow*, and, the past participle which is used here, means *grown*.

Crusher Fruits which have been ground to a pulp, or crushed, before pressing will yield larger quantities of juice. This is especially true of the hard fruit such as apples. Either the fruit can be treated on a pestle and mortar principle, by pounding the fruit with a heavy weight, or they can be 'put through the mangle'. This is a fairly accurate description of the action of a fruit crusher. They can be obtained commercially, or built by oneself.

Crust As a port matures the large amounts of tannins in it precipitate out to form a layer called the crust. In order to disturb this crust as little as possible, the bottle is marked with white paint to show its upper side. If moved, a port bottle should always be carried 'this way up'.

Cryptococcus One of the species of wild yeast which secretes mucus and so forms a slime in the must. Prevention of this infection is by sulphiting the must prior to adding the wine yeast. Should infection occur, sulphite is added at a concentration of 50–100 ppm, and the fermentation restarted after 24 hours.

Crystallisation The molecules of many chemical compounds can join together to form strange and beautiful shapes if their concentration is too high in a solution. This is experienced in winemaking if potassium tartrate crystallises out of solution to form argols.

Cultures of Yeast If an organism is grown under careful conditions in the laboratory so that only one particular species is present a pure culture is obtained. When speaking of a yeast culture it is always a pure strain that is meant. They should always be used to ferment wines.

Cup See Appendix XII.

Cuvée The name given to the blend of immature still wines which will be bottle fermented to produce Champagne.

Cuvée Close A method of producing sparkling wines commercially in large sealed vats. In these the second fermentation takes place. This is obviously a cheaper method than the traditional labour consuming one of bottle fermentation and is only used for the cheaper brands. Although possible for the amateur to emulate this method, it is dangerous, and requires equipment capable of withstanding high pressures.

Cylinders, Measuring Accurately calibrated measuring containers which are particularly useful in calculating blending proportions. The most useful sizes for the amateur winemaker are 10 ml and 100 ml.

Cytase The enzyme responsible for breaking down the starch in cereals.

— **D** —

Dame-Jeanne The French word for a carboy. From this word has been derived the English word *Demijohn*.

Damp Damp conditions are to be avoided in winemaking since any dampness within the winery will encourage the growth of moulds. Contrary to the belief of many people, a cellar ought not to be damp, but rather cool and dry, with maybe just a hint of moisture in the atmosphere.

Darkening Fruit, such as apples or pears, if cut and left exposed to the air, rapidly turn brown due to the action of an enzyme, o-polyphenoloxidase. This enzyme, if present, will survive fermentation and cause a darkening of the wine, known as oxidative casse.

Darkening due to Ascorbic Acid which is broken down to form brown coloured compounds. It has been suggested that the use of ascorbic acid as an anti-oxidant should be avoided in wines made with ascorbic acid containing ingredients (citrus fruit, parsnip, potato, currants, raspberries and gooseberries). (See Ascorbic Acid).

Daylight Spoilage See Actinic Action of Sunlight.

De-Amination Protein metabolism involves its breakdown to its constituent amino-acids. These in turn have the nitrogen containing group of atoms, or amine radicals, removed. This removal of nitrogen is called de-amination. In winemaking, the yeast requires protein building substances, and if these are not available there is a danger that the dead yeast cells will be broken down to provide some of the required nitrogen. This is a potentially dangerous situation, for, in the utilisation of the dead yeast, amyl alcohol is produced; and this is poisonous. It is to prevent this synthesis that nutrients should always be used in all recipes.

Débourbage The professional French term for sulphiting a must. The literal translation is *cleansing*.

Decanter Often of cut glass or crystal with silver mountings, they are as much table decorations as wine jugs.

Decanting Any wine with a sediment or crust in the bottle is best decanted before serving, both to increase its appeal and to prevent wastage due to stirring up of the débris. To do this, the bottle is removed from the bin and, keeping it on its side, the cork is drawn. The wine is then slowly run into the decanter, looking through the wine at a light source, traditionally a candle. When the sediment reaches the neck, pouring is stopped. Wines which commonly require decanting are port and the red wines rich in tannin, such as Hermitage.

Decinormal A chemical term to describe the strength of solutions of acids or alkalis. A decinormal solution contains one-tenth of the molecular weight per litre. (See Normal Solution).

Decolouring Any wine which is too dark in colour may be reduced in intensity by the use of decolouring agents such as charcoal or eggshell.

Dégorgement See Disgorging.

Demerara An unrefined cane sugar, brown in colour. It is of use in dessert wines where a golden colour is often required.

Demijohn A glass jar, usually with 'ears' below the neck, for ease of carrying. It has a nominal volume of one Imperial gallon, and is the newcomer to winemaking's basic unit for fermentation and bulk maturing.

Denaturing The structure of protein alters when acted on by heat or alcohol. The breakfast egg is a good example of denatured protein; when cooked it changes from runny and translucent to white and opaque. This phenomenon may occur when fortifying a wine which has apparently insufficient protein to cause a haze. After a few days, the fortified wine will show a haze which is positive to tests for protein. This is due to denaturing by the added alcohol. Cure is by normal methods of protein removal. (See Iso-Electric Point)

Density The density of a substance is its weight per unit volume; thus a heavy substance has a high density, and vice versa. Although a pound of feathers weighs the same as a pound of lead, the latter has a smaller volume and hence a higher density. Upon this principle is based the hydrometer, which works on the fact that a dense liquid can support more than a light liquid. (The common example given is that it is easier to float on the sea than in the bath.)

DEPC See Diethyl pyrocarbonate.

Depectinising Enzymes See Pectin entries.

Deposit Any fermentative process results in yeast débris and insoluble salts which fall to the bottom of the container to form a deposit, or lees. This process may go on for several years after the wine has finished fermenting, as the tannins gradually precipitate out of solution. This is especially true of red wines, and it is for this reason that red wines are not ready for bottling for a greater time than that required for white wine maturing. No wine should be allowed to rest on the deposit for more than two weeks after fermentation has finished. After that it should be racked every three months or so if a deposit forms. The exceptions to this are Champagne and sherry.

Designing Recipes rests on the ability to emulate the desired qualities of a wine. From a resting brief of the planned character, the recipe can be roughly drawn up and, after analysis of the ingredients, the final touches, such as acidity, gravity and required additives can be estimated and adjusted as necessary.

Dessert Fruits tend to be more fragrant, higher in sugar and lower in acid than their cooking counterparts and, when making wines from such ingredients, these points must be remembered and due allowance made.

Dessert Wine is intended for drinking at the end of a meal, often accompanying fruit. Accordingly, they tend to be higher in alcohol content, sweeter and with a fuller body than table wines. The colour is not important, except that it should be deep; and may be golden or brown, or one of the 'normal' shades. The bouquet must be pronounced, lest the dessert overpower the wine. Similarly, the flavour must be stronger than table wines.

Detergents Chemicals which, contrary to popular belief, are not only used for the washing up liquid! While they are invaluable for this, they can ruin a sparkling wine. This is because the way in which they remove dirt is by lowering the surface tension, thus making it more soluble. Due to this lowering of the surface tension the gas in a sparkling wine will escape rapidly. The solution is to ensure thorough rinsing after their use. The same is therefore best done despite claims to the contrary with detergents designed for the wine trade. At the same time this rinsing will prevent any taint that might arise due to their use, although they are claimed not to do so.

Determination of Constituents of Wine   See Test Entries.

Dextrans   are chains of sugars, shorter than starch chains. They are formed by the action of spoilage bacteria such as Leuconostoc. Prevention of this disorder, which may be recognised by a slimy deposit, is by sulphiting before fermentation. To cure the trouble, the wine is stirred and after sulphiting and settling the wine it can be racked and restarted.

Dextrins   are composed of medium-length chains of glucose and are usually present as the result of starch breakdown or partial destruction of pectins. If present, there will be a haze which may be difficult to clear. To determine the cause and, therefore, the partial cure see Diagnosis of fault, Appendix XI.

Dextrose   The old name for glucose, given because of its property of rotating polarised light to the right.

Dextrose Monohydrate   An expensive form of sugar, akin to invert sugar. Its use is not necessary since it is doubtful if its use confers any benefit on the wine. All that it will do is to remove one of the chemical steps in alcohol production (the hydrolysis of sucrose to its component sugars, glucose and fructose), which the yeast is quite capable of performing itself.

Diabetes   A disorder of sugar metabolism, common in man. A sufferer from this is always advised not to drink alcohol, but the occasional glass of *dry* wine is not unduly harmful.

Allow for the calorific value in the daily diet about 80 calories per 100 ml, and the carbohydrate content of 6 gms per cent.

Diabetic Wine While there is no such thing as a diabetic wine, a completely dry wine may be considered 'safe'. If required it may be sweetened with a non-fermentable substance such as sorbitol which is not metabolised in the human body.

Diacetyl A bitter-tasting substance produced by some of the lactobacilli, possibly by breakdown of some of the tannins. Prevention is by sulphiting the must prior to fermentation. Cure is sometimes possible by sweetening. Usually, however, the taste is not maskable and the wine should be discarded.

Diagnosis of Faults See Appendix XI.

Diammonium Phosphate The correct chemical name for Ammonium Phosphate.

Diastase An enzyme group which breaks down starch to maltose. This is secreted by grains and is liberated during mashing or malting. Thus it is of more importance to the brewer than the winemaker.

Dibasic An adjective applied to acids which have two hydrogen ions to liberate when that acid is put into solution. These ions are accepted by an alkali or base. Sulphuric acid is an example of a dibasic strong acid, while tartaric acid is the commonest dibasic weak acid met with in winemaking.

Diethyl Pyrocarbonate A compound which has a stabilising effect on wine by killing bacteria or yeasts present. In theory it should be the ideal stabilising agent because, like ethyl pyrocarbonate it is broken down to alcohol.

Diffusion All physical substances tend to pass from an area of high concentration to one of low concentration by diffusion. Yeast cells do not possess the ability to take in substances by chemical reactions, but can only do so if a substance is in solution and its molecular size is small enough to pass through the pores in the cell surface.

Dihydro-Acetate A hydrogen acceptor present at the beginning of fermentation before acetaldehyde is formed to take over this rôle. The acceptance of hydrogen ions by di-hydroxy acetone results in its reduction to glycerine.

Dilution A necessary step in the production of wines from most amateur ingredients to lessen factors such as over-acidity, overpowering flavour or bouquet. The amount of dilution depends on the initial assay of the juice extracted from the ingredients. Any dilution will in most cases lead to a low level of additives and ingredients, and this must be allowed for in calculations. Most commonly, this decrease is in the sugar and acidity levels, which must be corrected. All 'kit' wines require dilution of the concentrate in accordance with the instructions, but the levels of all ingredients have been adjusted to be correct in the final volume.

Dilution and Acidity If the volume of a fruit juice is doubled by adding water, it is obvious that the concentration of its constituents will be halved. Dilution of fruit juices is most often undertaken to lower an over-high acidity. If, after initial assay, the acidity of the juice is too high for the intended wine style, it is easy to work out by how much the juice needs to be diluted to bring it down to an acceptable level. The converse may be true; dilution may cause too low an acidity, in which case acid needs to be added.

Dilution and Alcohol When making a wine, there is always a loss of volume at racking time. To make this up entails adding either water with its consequential dilution of the alcohol, or, to prevent this, by using a topping-up wine. Another possibility is to make the wine stronger than its required strength. Dilutions after racking with tap water will then bring the level down to the planned strength.

Dilution and Colour White wines have no problems here, but if a deep red wine is wanted it is not a good idea to top up with water after racking, since it will dilute the colour. To avoid this, red wines should be made to a greater volume than the final jar, so that at each racking there will be either smaller or fewer jars.

Dilution and Flavour Dilution will result in less flavour. This can be useful in correcting an over-flavoured wine such as elderflower. Care must be taken with the diluent, but blending with a bland wine or a neutral topping-up wine should give a good result.

Dilution and Nutrients When starting a fermentation, it is nearly always of a smaller volume than the finished wine and it is necessary to allow for this when adding nutrients. Thus, add the recommended quantity per *final* gallon and not per initial gallon.

Dilution and Specific Gravity The effect of diluting any liquid is to lower its specific gravity. If one gallon of fluid with a specific gravity of 1200 is diluted to 2 gallons, the specific gravity will fall to 1100. Alternatively expressed, the gravity will be halved from 200 to 100. Allow for diluting to the final volume when adjusting the S.G. of the must.

Dinner Wines Usually with an alcohol content of 10 to 12 per cent, they should be chosen with the object of complementing the food. The snobbery of drinking wine x with menu a is to be deplored and choice should be on personal preference alone. Table wines usually have medium body and are dry or medium. The flavour must not be so overpowering as to mask the taste of the food.

Disaccharides These are sugars composed of two monosaccharides joined together. Sucrose (cane sugar) is made up of one molecule of glucose and one of fructose, and is the most important disaccharide in winemaking.

Discolouration See Colour of Wine; Dried Blood; Diagnosis of Faults, Appendix XI.

Disgorging The technique of removing yeast debris from sparkling wines following Rémuage. It is one of the most skilful manoeuvres in winemaking and entails the opening of an inverted bottle of sparkling wine whose neck has been cooled or frozen. The pressure of carbon dioxide in the bottle shoots out the plug of ice containing the yeast. The thumb is placed over the top of the bottle to prevent the loss of too much wine and the loss made up with syrup and brandy before sealing.

Disorders of Wine See Diagnosis of Faults, Appendix XI.

Dissociation The characteristic of an acid in solution, when it splits into its constituent parts which, by definition, must include hydrogen ions.

Distillation of Spirits *is totally illegal without a licence from H.M. Customs.* It involves heating alcohol to such a temperature that water and certain of the substances which are toxic in any appreciable concentration (such as fusel oils) are separated from the alcohol and bouquet-conferring esters, known as congenerics. If distillation is attempted without proper equipment there is a real danger that the poisonous substances present will be concentrated by the process and not driven off. (See Duty; Law; Fractionating; Fortification).

Dom Perignon A monk of the Benedictine order in the 17th century credited for first using cork to seal wine bottles and thereby showing the way to the production of vintage wines, for, without a sure method of protection, the wine will become infected. His memory is hallowed in the Champagne which bears his name.

Dosage The French term used by champagne producers to describe the technique of adding the mixture of cane sugar, wine and spirit to Champagne after dégorgement.

Doubling Up The technique used to restart a stuck ferment. A fresh yeast starter is prepared and once active is added to about an equal volume of stuck wine (after racking). When this is fermenting, the volume of wine in the fermentation jar is doubled. Each time the ferment is active the volume is increased until all the wine is restarted.

Doux The French word meaning *sweet*, which is often used on the label to describe such a wine.

Dried Blood A fining agent formerly used widely by commercial vignerons. It is not recommended for amateurs, since over-fining which causes discoloration is easy.

Dried Flowers are a convenient way of using flowers all the year round. They do not produce quite the same bouquet as their fresh counterparts. Broadly speaking, 1 oz of dried flowers is approximately equal to ½ gallon of fresh flowers, with the exception of elderflowers, where 1 oz dried equals 1 gallon of the fresh flowers.

Dried Fruit cannot be processed by pulping or pressing techniques such as are used for the majority of fruits. They have to be rehydrated so that sugars and flavourings can be leached out. Sterilisation is essential since they tend to have a high micro-organism population. The possible methods of extraction are either to boil the dried fruit for about ½ hour, or to pour boiling water over the fruit and press. When the temperature has dropped below 85°F, sulphite is added to sterilise the must. Pulp fermentation is valuable with dried fruit since it allows a longer time to extract as much flavour and colour as is required by the action of alcohol as it is formed.

Dried Malt The main use of dried malt to the winemaker is in the preparation of starter mixtures. There are also recipes which include this ingredient.

Dried Yeast One of the basic forms in which yeast can be purchased. To make a starter, simply add the recommended amount to the starter solution.

Drosophila Melanogaster The fruit or vinegar fly is attracted by the scent of fermentation and, since it is one of the carriers of acetomonas, it will, if allowed access to the must, cause acetification. (A good reason to use an airlock!) Furthermore, it is advisable to use sulphite in the airlock since the flies may get into the lock and, unless the bacteria are killed, may still infect the wine.

Dry Wine is defined as a wine which tastes dry to the palate.

Unfortunately, this simple glib definition does not cater for the sweet tooth! With the recent introduction of Dextrocheck and Quantan, to the amateur winemaker's analysis kit the proposal has been made that a wine should be considered dry if it has less than 1 per cent sugar on testing with this method.

Dryness is detected by the lack of sugar on tasting a wine. This should not be confused with astringency, detected by a dryness in the mouth, due to tannin.

Dustbins, Plastic are excellent containers for pulp fermentation if made of a hard plastic. The colour is not important now that cadmium has been cleared of a charge of being leached out of yellow plastics in toxic amounts. The important considerations are a great enough capacity; a tight fitting lid; and the colour will not leach out when in contact with alcohol. This last is not likely to occur if a hard plastic is used, such as those of a food grade. Do not use black dustbins, as they are usually soft.

Duty Perhaps the rudest word in the winemaker's vocabulary! H.M. Customs and Excise levy a fixed tax or duty on all alcohol sold in this country. Thus, while it is permissible (and expected!) to give wines to friends, it is not allowed to sell them. This includes the donating of wines to charitable purposes such as bring and buy sales or raffle competitions. (See Law)

— **E** —

Earthenware See Containers, Earthenware

Ebullioscope The expensive professional way of measuring alcohol accurately enough to satisfy the tax man who charges according to alcohol level down to the second decimal point.

Edelfäuse The German name for Botrytis cinerea.

Effervescence The phenomenon seen when a bottle of sparkling wine is opened. The carbon dioxide under pressure in the wine, in trying to escape, causes fizzing. A lively degree of effervescence is a required feature of a sparkling wine, and it should continue to bubble slowly for a long time after opening. (See Ethyl Pyrocarbonate).

Egg Spoon See Appendix XII.

Egg White See Albumin; Albuminous Protein.

Eggshell Save the breakfast eggshell and, after cleaning and baking, powder it. As well as decolouring the wine, it will aid clearing.

Egrappoir A machine for stripping grapes from their stems. By using it, the bitter tannins in the stems and pips are not crushed and therefore tannin extraction is minimised.

Elder From the elder tree comes a harvest to suit every winemaker. The leaves, flowers and berries, white or red, can all be used to make country or blended wines.

Elderberry The elderberry, fresh or dried, is the pre-eminent amateur winemaking ingredient for basing red wines. The quantities required vary between 1–4 lb per gallon fresh; while 1 lb dried fruit will suffice for up to 5–6 gallons, depending on the blend of ingredients used. The fruit require scalding with boiling water, or sulphiting, to kill the bloom and insect population. Juice or pulp fermentation is possible with elderberries, but to obtain a deep colour the latter is better. Elderberries tend to be low in acid and so careful acid analysis and correction is needed, preferably with tartaric and malic acids. The tannin content of elderberries is high enough for the wine to withstand long cask maturing. If desired, after completing the pulp fermentation, the unpressed marc can be reconstituted with acid and sugar and a rosé wine made. Nearly all elderberry wines need long maturing to allow the tannin content to fall to a palatable level.

Elderflower Depending on the selected tree, it is possible to produce wines which vary from repellant to delightful. Any tree which smells pleasant is likely to be safe from the catty bouquet so often obtained from elderflowers. Approximately 1 pint per gallon is needed of the fresh flowers, or about $\frac{1}{2}$ oz per gallon of the dried. Since many of the German white wines are said to have an elderflower-like bouquet, their use in a must intended for a hock type wine is recommended.

Elderflower for Bouquet Many fruits, or vegetables, while being good ingredients for body or vinosity, are poor in bouquet producing esters. To combat this deficiency, elderflowers are one of the best ingredients available. About ½ pint of fresh flowers, or ¼ oz of dried flowers per gallon, is adequate.

Electrical Charge Many substances carry electrical charges. These are either positive or negative. If a solution contains particles which have the same electrical charge they will tend to form a colloid, since the charged particles will be repelled from each other. To clear a wine with a colloidal haze depends on choosing an oppositely charged substance. (See Bentonite).

Ellagic Acid One of the tannins. It is responsible for most of the bitterness conferred by the tannin group on a wine.

Endomycopsis One of the yeasts capable of breaking down starch by means of the enzyme amylase which it secretes. It is not, however, a wine yeast.

Energy Transfer No chemical reaction takes place without energy being used or released. In winemaking, the phosphate radical is the major energy releaser. Energy is stored in this radical from reactions which give off energy and, when required in reactions, the phosphate gives up its energy.

Enolase One of the enzymes secreted by yeasts. Its function is to break down glyceric acid to pyruvic acid. Like most enzymes, it acts on only one reaction.

Enzymes Organic catalysts produced by living cells. They do not depend on the cell for their livelihood, but can perform their reactions outside the cell. Most fermentative reactions take place outside the cell. Unlike inorganic catalysts enzymes are destroyed by boiling and inactivated by freezing, (the principle behind deep freezing foods). Many enzymes require a co-enzyme to act as an energy provider for the reaction, or as hydrogen acceptors in oxidative reactions. Some metals act as activators for enzymes which explains the need for calcium and magnesium in the must.

Enzyme, Oxidative Fruit, especially if over-ripe, have a high concentration of an enzyme, o-polyphenoloxidase, which oxidises tannin to a brown coloured substance. To prevent this, only sound fruit should be used and sulphited immediately after preparation. (See Casse, Oxidative).

Enzyme, Pectin destroying See Pectin destroying Enzymes.

Enzyme, Starch destroying See Amylase.

Enzymes and Temperature The rate at which a chemical reaction takes place is usually doubled by raising the temperature by 10°C. This theory, however, does not work with enzymes since with increasing temperature despite an increase in the reaction rate, there is also an increase in the rate at which protein is denatured. Thus, by striking a balance between speed of reaction and speed of denaturing, one can arrive at an optimum temperature. This, for wine yeasts, is about 70°F, (21°C).

Epsom Salts Another name for magnesium sulphate crystals.

Equipment The choice of equipment is a matter of pocket, personal preference and must be based on the amount of wine produced per year.

Equipment, Basic The initial equipment need only consist of the following: 1 gallon bucket, 1 gallon jar with bored cork and air-lock, racking tube and the ingredients for the first gallon of wine. From this beginning further equipment can be purchased as required, e.g. hydrometer, siphons, funnels, sieve, test equipment, bottles and corks, etc.

Equipment, Cleaning See Sterilising entries.

Essences blended with a fortified, neutral base wine, can simulate most of the commercial aperitifs and liqueurs.

Esters are produced by the condensation of an acid and an alcohol. They are sweet-smelling compounds and are responsible for most of the flavour of a wine. Some esters are obtained from ingredients and, since they are volatile, boiling should not be used for flavour extraction if possible. Other and more important esters are produced during the reduction reactions that take place in the bottle, For a good bouquet and flavour, succinic and malic acid esters are important. Some of the former is produced during fermentation, but the wine will benefit if additional succinic acid is added prior to maturation. Apart from the right blend of ingredients time is essential to obtain a good flavour and bouquet and it is for this reason (as well as tannin reduction in red wines), that wines should be allowed at least one year's maturing before drinking.

Estufagem The room in which madeira is 'cooked' at high temperatures for periods dependent on the final quality of the wine. The lower the temperature and greater the time, the higher the quality. This heating process causes caramelisation (or Maderisation) of the residual sugar.

Ethanol The proper chemical name for Ethyl Alcohol.

Ethyl Alcohol See Alcohol, Ethyl.

Ethyl Acetate An ester which has the smell of peardrops. It is produced when a wine acetifies.

Ethyl Pyrocarbonate is an unstable compound formed when bottle fermentation occurs. It is formed by the joining of alcohol and carbon dioxide. On opening the bottle the rate of loss of carbon dioxide (or rate of bubble formation is inversely proportional to the concentration of ethyl pyrocarbonate. Thus a good sparkling wine retains its 'fizz' for a long time because the bubbles can only form as the decomposition of ethyl pyrocarbonate takes place.

Evaporation The principle on which the production of fruit concentrates is based. By boiling off the water in a vacuum, the volatile esters are retained.

Excise See Duty; Fortification; Fractionating; Law.

Exhibiting Wines See Competitions.

Exponential Feeding A system of sugar additions to a must so that a high alcohol content can be achieved. If all the sugar is added at the start of fermentation, there is a great danger that the sugar will inhibit or even kill the yeast. By adding small amounts of sugar each time the specific gravity falls to 1·005, the yeast 'learns' to tolerate alcohol concentrations which normally would kill it. In this way, a slow, steady ferment is encouraged. This aids quality by not causing the vaporisation of esters.

Extraction by Alcohol Tannins and many of the natural pigments are insoluble in water. To overcome this, ingredients rich in such compounds are left in contact with the must until sufficient extraction has been obtained. This is necessary with berried fruit, currants, dried fruit, flowers, gooseberries, grain, grapes, leaves and stone fruit. (See Alcohol, Colour Extraction; Pulp Fermentation)

Extraction by Boiling is used for vegetables, dried fruit and a few others as a means of flavour extraction. Recipe instructions must be followed carefully and the boiling time not exceeded, otherwise hazes will form and may be difficult to clear and a cooked flavour may be given to the wine. Flowers should never be boiled, as the steam generated will drive off the volatile aromatic esters which are exactly the part of the flower required.

Extraction, Chemical This includes all methods of extraction involving the addition of substances such as enzymes and sulphite. It does not, however, include alcoholic leaching of compounds which, correctly speaking, it should.

Extraction by Cold Water Other than sugars, there are few winemaking substances which are soluble in water. However, the use of cold water is preferable to hot, since the latter causes volatilisation of many of the aromatics present in the ingredients. Used in conjunction with enzymes and sulphite, and pulp fermentation, if indicated, this system will cover the preparation of most basic ingredients, with the exception of vegetables. In using cold water, care is required to avoid infection, by the adequate use of sulphite, until fermentation is active.

Extraction of Colour See Colour Extraction.

Extraction of Juice Following the pulping or crushing of fruit, the juice can be extracted by pressing. The yield can be increased by the use of cellulose enzymes.

Extraction and Metabisulphite See Sulphite and Extraction.

Extraction by Pectic Enzymes See Pectic Enzymes and Extraction.

Extraction by Pressing is a purely physical method. By applying pressure to the fruit pulp, the juice trapped between the particles is expressed. Do not over-press, since the last pressings are high in tannins. Also the fruit pulp may come over into the wine with a consequential loss of quality.

Extraction by Pulp Fermentation See Extraction by Alcohol; Extraction of Colour; Fermentation, Pulp.

Extraction by Steam See Steam Extraction.

Extraction by Soaking See Extraction by Cold Water.

Extractors are pieces of equipment designed to facilitate the obtaining of juice from fruit and to increase this yield. They can work on the principles of either pressure or steam.

— F —

Facultative Anaerobe An organism which can survive and multiply either with or without oxygen. The fact that yeasts belong to this group of organisms enables us to produce alcohol. In the absence of air yeast changes its metabolic pathways and produces alcohol as its final metabolite; in other words, alcohol is a waste product of anaerobic metabolism.

Fahrenheit The temperature scale at present being phased out in favour of the centigrade scale. On the Fahrenheit scale, freezing point is 32° and boiling point is 212°. (See Appendix XII.)

Faults See Diagnosis of Faults, Appendix XI.

Feeding of Yeast See Exponential Feeding.

Fehling's Solution A pair of reagents which, when added to a solution, estimates the sugar content colorimetrically. Its use is being superseded by Clinitest tablets.

Fermentable Base Any carbohydrate capable of entering the fermentation pathway and being metabolised by yeast enzymes to alcohol. This, in addition to sugar, natural or added, includes some pectin and starch degraded by the commercial enzymes used in preparing the must.

Fermentation is nature's incinerator. It is, for the winemaker, a controlled example of many processes occurring in nature by which dead materials are broken down to their component elements to become available for recycling. It always requires the presence of yeast and their enzymes. Most fermentative processes in nature are aerobic, but the winemaker has, over the centuries, learnt that by excluding air the sugars are broken down to alcohol.

Fermentation See: Additives;
Aerobic Fermentation;
A.cohol Yield from Fermentation;
Anaerobic Fermentation;
Bottle Fermentation;
By-products of Fermentation.

Fermentation, Conditions required Assuming the correct balance of ingredients, it is not enough just to add yeast and hope that a wine will emerge.

(a) **Additives** including citric acid are needed to ensure a healthy ferment.
(b) **Oxygen** is needed to encourage the establishment of a healthy yeast colony prior to anaerobic fermentation.
(c) **Temperature** See Temperature and Fermentation.
(d) **Sterility** is essential to prevent infection.

Fermentation, Conduction of The stages to be performed in the production of a wine are:

(1) Prepare yeast starter.
(2) Clean and sterilise equipment.
(3) Prepare and sterilise juice.
(4) Analyse and adjust acidity, pH, Specific Gravity, sugar and volume.
(5) Innoculate yeast.
(6) Control of temperature; and feeding during fermentation.
(7) Rack at end of fermentation.
(8) Mature.

Fermentation Enzymes Without enzymes yeasts could not produce alcohol. Their function is to aid the reactions involved in the metabolism of the yeast cell. Each enzyme has its own reaction to catalyse; and there are four groups of enzymes which are of importance in winemaking.

(a) **Sugar Enzymes** which break down sugars to their simplest forms. ie Invertase breaks down sucrose to fructose and maltose.
(b) **Alcohol Enzymes** which speed the reactions which convert sugar to alcohol
(c) **Protein Enzymes** which break down proteins to their constituent amino-acids.
(d) **Oxidising Enzymes** which can cause over-oxidation.

Fermentation, Glycolysis The series of reactions which result in glucose and fructose being broken down to pyruvic acid, and alcohol being formed from this. The complete series of reactions are given, together with their enzymes, in Appendix **IX**.

Fermentation Inhibitors The continued life of yeast cells depends on sufficient nutrients and sugar, and the non-poisoning of enzyme systems. The osmotic pressure must be less than that required to rupture the cell wall. To stop fermentation one can either add only enough foodstuffs to reach a predetermined alcohol level or one can stop fermenting chemically. To do this, it is necessary to inhibit the enzyme systems so that the yeast cell can no longer break down sugars to provide itself with energy. The simple physical method of stopping fermentation is to rack the wine at short intervals so that the yeast colony is gradually reduced in size until no more alcohol is produced. At the same time, the addition of sulphite will temporarily inhibit the yeast so that the remaining cells do not have a chance to re-establish themselves. A second racking will almost entirely eliminate yeast from the immature wine. The peel of citrus fruit contains oils which, by forming a layer on the surface of the wine, will effectively prevent a young colony from establishing itself. (See Benzoic Acid; Diethyl Pyrocarbonate; Potassium Sorbate; Sorbic Acid).

Fermentation, Juice This is the fermentation of an extract without pulp. An ingredient which does not have easily expressible juice, e.g. leaves, is prepared in the recommended manner for that plant. After assay and addition of nutrients, the yeast is added, but at no time does that ingredient come into contact with the yeast. Ingredients which are suitable for juice fermentation are: vegetables, soft fruit and citrus fruit.

Fermentation, Lag Phase is the period between the time the yeast is added to a must and the time fermentation becomes obvious. During this phase, the yeast cells are dividing and utilising the oxygen dissolved in the must. When the oxygen is exhausted the cells cease aerobic and begin anaerobic fermentation, and at this time the fermentation becomes obvious.

Fermentation Locks   See Airlock.

Fermentation, Malo-Lactic   See Malo-Lactic Reaction.

Fermentation Management   See Fermentation, Conduction of

Fermentation Pathways See Appendices IX and X.

Fermentation, Phases of See Fermentation, Lag Phase; Fermentation, Primary; Fermentation, Secondary.

Fermentation and Phosphates See Ammonium Phosphate; Energy Transfer; Phosphates; Potassium Phosphate.

Fermentation under Pressure is normally encountered in the bottle or tank process of champagne making. It is not to be undertaken by the amateur without special equipment and great care. Most yeasts are inhibited by the presence of carbon dioxide above a pressure of more than a few p.s.i., but champagne yeast is capable of and required to work at great pressures of carbon dioxide.

Fermentation, Primary is the first vigorous fermentation seen a few hours after yeast innoculation, when foaming often occurs due to the large volumes of gas given off. It usually lasts a few days, after which fermentation quietens down. During this time no volatile substances such as flowers should be added, as they are in danger of being 'boiled' off by the carbon dioxide.

Fermentation, Pulp is the utilisation of fermentation to extract colour and flavouring from ingredients by their solubility in the alcohol produced in the first few days of fermentation. To achieve this, the cleaned ingredients, some of the sugar and additives are placed in about half of the final volume of the wine. The yeast is added and, when the desired depth of colour and flavour is reached, the fruit is strained from the juice and pressed. Pulp fermentation is advocated for dried fruit, dark red fruit, berries and stone fruit.

Fermentation, Second The re-fermentation in the bottle, which gives a sparkling wine its sparkle.

Fermentation, Secondary This is the period of fermentation from the time the fermentation settles down after the initial phase to the end of fermentation. There is no difference chemically between the primary and secondary ferments. It is merely the rates of fermentation which distinguishes them. Ideally, there should be a long, slow secondary ferment to ensure quality. This is emphasised by the fact that floral esters added during the first stage are likely to be volatilised, but if added at the start of the second they will remain to enhance the wine.

Fermentation, Spontaneous Any sugar containing solution, if left in contact with the open air, is likely to become infected with yeasts. As all yeasts are capable by definition of fermentation, such a liquid will become alcoholic. However, the chances of a suitable yeast infecting the must are minute—almost as small as the chances of spoilage are great. Therefore, for winemaking do not, whatever the recipe says, rely on luck: use a proper wine yeast.

Fermentation, Stages of See Fermentation, Lag Phase; Fermentation, Primary and Fermentation, Secondary.

Fermentation, Sticking See Sticking *et seq*.

Fermentation and Temperature See Temperature and Fermentation.

Fermentation, Theory of In the simplest chemical terms, one molecule of sugar is converted to two molecules of alcohol and two molecules of carbon dioxide, by the action of the yeast enzymes. Behind this statement lies a large number of chemical reactions. (See Glycolysis, Appendix IX).

Fermentation Trap See Airlock.

Film Yeast A common cause of infection in a wine. The infection starts as small islands of white on the surface of the wine which gradually increase in size until the surface of the wine is covered with a whitish skin or pellicle. The effect of a film yeast is to convert the alcohol to carbon dioxide and water, and, therefore, once diagnosed, cure is urgently needed. By stirring, the pellicle is broken up, and sulphiting will kill the organisms. The wine is then racked after a few days. Prevention is by hygiene and anaerobic conditions. If however, a sherry type wine is being made, do not break the flor.

Filter Funnel Any funnel with a folded filter paper or filter medium contained with a plug of cotton wool will serve as a filter funnel. Its function is purely to retain the filter medium and deposit. For winemaking, filter papers tend to be too slow.

Filter Paper one of the possible media for use in filtering a wine. Their use in open funnels is taking an unnecessary risk with over-oxidation, especially as there are more efficient methods available.

Filter Pulp See Asbestos; Cellulose.

Filter, Rapid Another generic name for continuous filters.

Filter, Vacuum has the advantage of speeding filtration. Using a Bucchner flask and funnel with a normal filter medium, a partial vacuum is applied across the filter pad by sucking out the flask with a vacuum pump.

Filtration A wine which does not clear on its own after about a year and shows no signs of doing so will need fining and filtering. Filtering involves the removal of suspended particles from a fluid by passing both through a medium composed of a substance with pores large enough to allow the liquid to pass but small enough to entrap the suspended particles. In winemaking, the usual filtration requirements are to remove yeast debris and the larger solids deposited but not to remove the molecules responsible for colour, flavour and bouquet.

Filtration and Asbestos In view of the dangers of its use, it is far better to use safe filter media such as cellulose. These work just as well and are not so liable to cause taints or lightening in the wine.

Filtration and Cellulose This non-toxic substance, and powders allied to it, have taken the place of asbestos as filter media. To use the pads or powders, the instructions given with them are followed. The first washings should be discarded in case they taint the wine with a filter paper taste.

Filtration, Continuous Until recently filtration involved the laborious task of filling funnels at irregular intervals as the fluid levels dropped, but, with the advent of continuous filters, this hazardous job has been obviated. All the available filters are easy to use, hygienic and, above all, safe in producing clear wine when the instructions are followed.

Filtration and Oxidation As in every stage of winemaking undertaken in the presence of air, there is a high risk of over-oxidation. This is especially true of filtration via funnels. On the other hand, closed filtration such as is achieved by the kit filters, is obviously less prone to the problem. As with bottling, a wine develops a similar sickness after filtration from which it recovers after a few weeks. It is possible to create an oxygen-free atmosphere for filtration by filling the receiving jar and filtration equipment with carbon dioxide from an actively fermenting jar.

Final Specific Gravity The specific gravity of the wine when fermentation has finished.

Fining The technique of adding substances to the wine to aid clearing. Most stubborn hazes are colloidal in nature and most fining agents are also colloidal. They act by neutralising the electrical charges on the haze forming particles, so that they fall out of solution.

Fining Agent Any compound added to a wine to aid clearing. The common agents are dealt with under their respective headings: Albumin; Bentonite; Casein; Gelatine; Metabisulphite; Tannin.

Fining Agents, Action of See Colloid; Iso-electric Point; Sulphite and Clearing; Tannin and Clarification.

Fining, Choice of Method Except in the use of bentonite, there is a danger of over-fining, and it is best, in order to avoid this, to perform a trial fining. Bentonite is the safest agent; after which comes a gelatin-tannin mixture. Usually one of these two methods will clear a wine but, if not, one of the other methods will be tried until at least a partial success is achieved.

Fining Technique After a trial fining, the chosen agent is mixed to the right proportions and this is added to part of the wine and fully dispersed or dissolved as the case may be. This is then added to the bulk of the wine. After a week or so in a cool place, the wine will probably be clear and may then be racked off the deposit and maturation continued in the normal manner.

Fining, Trial Before attempting to clear a large volume of wine, it is important to test it to see which method of fining (and at what concentration) will give the best result. Failure to do so may well end in an over-fined wine in which the haze may be permanent. To perform a trial fining, prepare a series of beakers having a known volume of wine in them (50 or 100 ml is usual). To each of these is added $\frac{1}{2}$, 1, $1\frac{1}{2}$, 2, $2\frac{1}{2}$ etc. ml of 1 per cent test solution (1 gm in 100 ml). After 24–48 hours, look for the container with the smallest amount of fining giving the clearest wine. The usual first trial is Bentonite and, if this fails, a tannin-gelatin system should be tried, and this will usually give a satisfactory result. From the amount of finings giving the best result, the total weight per gallon can be calculated.

Fish Gelatine See Isinglass.

Flaming When removing yeast from a container, sterility is essential. The neck of the container is sterilised by passing it quickly through the tip of a flame. If using a platinum loop, the loop must also be flamed before picking up yeast from an agar slope.

Flatness in a wine has several meanings, depending on the authority consulted. It may mean under acidity, lack of tannin, too little alcohol, or the wine may be too old. Thus it would appear to be a term to be avoided without defining the meaning. So, why not just describe the fault?

Flavour The term used for the taste of a wine. In describing a flavour, it is important to describe what is tasted in terms understood by others. So, rather than using esoteric terms, relate the taste to a known food, flavour, etc.

Flavour, Medicinal The tangy taste to a wine which has too little acid. To prevent this fault it is important to add the correct amount of acid at the start. Once present, this off-flavour is impossible to erradicate.

Flavour, Metallic When a metal taints a wine it imparts a distinctive metallic taste to the wine. To prevent this the wine should not be allowed into contact with any metal other than stainless steel or aluminium. Once present, a metallic taste is impossible to remove by amateur techniques.

Flavourings There are now many varieties of extracts and flavourings on the market with which it is possible to simulate most liqueurs and aperitifs.

Fly, Fruit See Drosophila Melanogaster.

Fly, Vinegar See Drosophila Melanogaster.

Flogger The simplest corking equipment. It consists of a flat piece of wood with which corks are hammered home into the bottle until flush with the neck.

Flor The Spanish word meaning flower. To the winemaker it is the growth of yeast on the surface of a wine intended as a sherry. Its growth is a matter of chance even to the professional. After racking a sherry into an 'open' cask the growth of a flor is encouraged by the massive amounts of oxygen reaching the yeast together with the correctly balanced wine. Often only a few isolated patches of yeast grow which, while not preventing oxidation to the extent of a complete flor, still influences the final flavour of the wine, giving it a definite sherry taste. Beneath a complete flor the wine does not darken but remains pale. Oxidation is prevented by the yeast taking up all the oxygen entering the cask.

Flor Formation, Conditions for Although the chemistry of flor formation is not yet fully understood, a few facts are known to influence its growth. The conditions favouring the development of a commercial flor are:

Alcohol content	...	14·5–15 per cent
pH	...	3·1–3·4
Tannin ...	...	less than 0·03 mgs per cent
Sugar	...	less than 150 mgs per cent
Sulphur dioxide	...	100 ppm

The maturing vessel should not have more than 24 inches of wine in it, with ideally, at least half as much space again for ullage.

Flor Composition See Yeast, Sherry.

Flowers are the reproductive parts of plants which can be recognised by the presence of sepals (green, 'under petals'), petals, stamens (spike-like structures in the centre) and ovaries (seedpods). Their attraction to the winemaker is the scent they carry and which is used to add bouquet to a wine. On their own they make poor wines, as they are lacking in nutrients and vinous qualities. However, when used with other ingredients, they are an important item in many recipes.

Flowers, Boiling *Do not boil flowers.* Because most esters are volatile, boiling flowers will drive off the most important constituent—the aroma.

Flowers for Bouquet See Bouquet, Flowers for.

Flowers, Preparation of Flowers do not contain much juice, so it is obvious that juice fermentation is not practical. Therefore, some modified form of pulp fermentation is needed. Like all natural produce flowers contain a large population of unwanted insects and bacteria. The insects can be removed by washing with *cold* water. The bacteria will be inhibited by proper conditions in the must. After about a week, when the primary ferment is over, flowers may be added. To add them sooner is to incur the same risks as boiling. When sufficient aroma has been extracted the flowers are removed from the must. To make this easier, the flowers can be placed in a bag prior to inclusion in the must.

Flower Wines Unblended, flowers produce thin wines with a good bouquet. Since they contain little nitrogen it is vital to add plenty of nutrients. To overcome the problem of thinness, vinosity must be added either as raisins or grape concentrate. Flowers are also low in acid and tannin, and these must also be included.

Flowers of Wine   Or Mycoderma aceti. (See Acetobacter).

Formic Acid   is the simplest of the organic acids, and is produced in small amounts during fermentation. Most of this is oxidised to carbonic acid to form part of the buffer system of the wine.

Fortification   is the only legal way in which the alcohol content of a wine may be increased by amateurs. It is done by adding a wine or spirit of a higher alcoholic strength to the base wine. It is a very expensive procedure and should be reserved for exceptional wines, or when making one's own liqueurs.

Fortification Calculation   The Pearson square has long been the standard arithmetical method of calculating spirit additions. This can be stated more simply as:

$$\frac{\text{Volume of spirit required}}{} = \frac{\text{Volume of wine (intended—actual strength)}}{\text{(spirit strength—intended strength)}}$$

The alcoholic strengths are in weight/volume % or proof °, but it is important not to mix the units.

Fortification, Equipment needed   Apart from a 100 ml calibrated jar, the equipment needed is that for alcohol determination.

Fortified Spirit   The commonly used fortifying spirits are vodka or brandy. The former is widely used in the form of 140% Polish spirit. Brandy is used commercially in the fortification of champagne and port.

Fouloir   The French word meaning a Grape Press.

Fractionating   (or separating a solution into its component substances). The methods used are either those of distillation or freezing point differences. Alcohol both boils and freezes at a lower temperature than water. Thus by applying heat or cold to separate the two, the alcohol concentration can be raised. *This is illegal without an excise licence.*

Freezing Mixture To reduce the pressure as well as to freeze a plug of wine containing yeast before dégorgement, the neck of the bottle should be placed in a mixture of ice, salt and water. Alternatively, if available, carbon dioxide snow can be used instead of ice.

Frizzante The Italian word meaning a sparkling wine.

Fructose A hexose monosaccharide, one molecule of which together with one molecule of glucose forms the disaccharide sucrose. After inversion, the yeast can metabolise the fructose to alcohol. Sauternes yeast is interesting in that it metabolises fructose more quickly than glucose, unlike most other wine yeasts where the converse is true.

Fruit Botanically, they are the female or seed-bearing parts of a plant. To the housewife or winemaker they are the edible parts of many plants, trees or bushes.

Fruit, Acidity of See Acidity of Fruit.

Fruit, Bloom of See Bloom of Fruit.

Fruit Fly See Drosophila Melanogaster.

Fruit Juice All plants have some juice in them, but, for the winemaker, fruit are considered juicy only if easily expressed in largish volumes (i.e. citrus fruit have juice, while bananas do not). Depending on the volume of expressible juice, the method of fermentation is decided.

Fruit, Preparation of Fresh fruit should be used as soon as possible. Failure to do so will allow the wild yeasts on their surface to start fermenting and rot the fruit. The stages in preparing fruit are: washing, stoning (if needed), chopping, pressing, sterilising and then blending with other ingredients.

Fruit Pressing Depending on fruit used, wine style intended and fermentation method selected, the timing of pressing will vary. Most fruit have some free run juice (the juice obtainable when the skin is broken). On the other hand, the marc will contain large volumes trapped between the particles of fruit. To obtain this juice, the fruit are pressed. The technique is simple—the fruit is compressed until the juice runs. When all the juice has flowed from the first press, increase the pressure. Do not put on maximum pressure at the start, as this will wreck the press and lessen the yield. Do not overpress fruit. The last pressings do not make quality wines, often due to the tannins and glycosides which are not extracted until the pips and twigs are pressed.

Fruit Pulp is prepared by shredding fruit in a pulper or mincer (providing it is not made of a haze-producing metal). The pressing of pulp rather than the whole fruit will yield a greater volume of juice.

Fruit Types Taking 'fruit', incorrectly, to include *all* ingredients. See Elder; Grain; Hard Fruit; Herbs; Leaf; Rhubarb; Soft Fruit; Vegetables.

Fruit Wines Any non-poisonous fruit can be used to make wine, either on its own or as a blend. The method of preparation, fermentation and the style of wine depends on the type of fruit selected.

Fungus A simple plant characterised by the lack of chlorophyll. One class, the Ascomycetes, contains the yeasts. Fungi obtain their foodstuffs from the soil but, not being able to synthesise sugar from carbon dioxide and sunlight (photosynthesis), have instead the ability to break down sugars with the enzymes they secrete. It is this ability the winemaker uses when he makes wine, together with the other strange property yeasts have, which is not only to survive, but to flourish in the absence of oxygen and as a by-product of anaerobic metabolism to produce alcohol.

Funnel A simple, basic piece of equipment to simplify the pouring of liquids through narrow openings. Since they vary in size from a few inches upwards, one of the correct size can be selected to do the job.

Funnel, Buchner See Buchner Funnel.

Fusel Oils are higher alcohols. They are produced as a by-product of fermentation by breakdown of some of the amino-acids from autolysing yeasts. The nitrogen thus obtained enables the reproducing yeasts to build up their own protein. To prevent the formation of too much fusel oil, nutrients should always be used when preparing the must. Ingredients which are most likely to cause high levels of fusel oils are potatoes and cereals. In trace concentration, they add flavour and bouquet, but in amounts greater than this they cause hangovers at best and convulsions which can lead to death at worst.

— **G** —

Galactonuric Acid A weak acid which forms long chain polymers which, when esterified with methyl alcohol, becomes *pectin*.

Galactose A sugar which is of importance to the milk-drinker! One molecule each of galactose and glucose form lactose—the sugar of milk. This sugar is used in winemaking to sweeten wines, since wine yeasts cannot metabolise it.

Gallic Acid One of the tannins. Together with catechol and ellagic acid it is responsible for most of the astringency in a red wine. As it readily combines with gelatine, it follows that fining with this agent will remove this acid and produce a smoother softer wine.

Gallon The basic unit for winemaking in this country and the U.S.A. Care must be taken between the different volumes of the Imperial and U.S. Gallons.

Gallon, Imperial is composed of 8 pints, each of 20 fluid ounces. 1 gallon Imperial equals 1·2 U.S. gallons; and 4·5 litres.

Gallon, U.S. consists of 8 pints, each of 16 fluid ounces. 1 gallon U.S. equals 0·83 Imperial gallons; and 3·78 litres.

Galvanised Iron is made by dipping clean iron into molten zinc. This zinc covering forms carbonates by reactions with the atmospheric carbon dioxide. Since carbonates are soluble salts, they will dissolve if in contact with an acid medium, such as wine. Apart from causing hazes, the use of such containers is to be deprecated, as zinc is a toxic metal.

Gas A chemical state, in which an element or compound is in a fluid state. Unlike liquids, gases have no definite shape or volume. They are all soluble to some degree in water; hence tap water contains oxygen which can be utilised by an unestablished yeast colony.

Gay Lussac A French chemist who was the first to hypothesise the fermentation equation: one molecule of sugar yields two molecules each of alcohol and carbon dioxide. Also the name given to the Continental scale of alcohol content. 1 per cent alcohol equals 1 degree Gay Lussac.

Gelatine A protein obtained from animal collagen. Its use in winemaking is as a fining agent. A 1 per cent solution is used. In making the solution, do not over-heat the gelatin or it will be denatured. Trial fining is essential to avoid over-fining which causes discoloration, off-flavours and hazes. Gelatin combines with tannin to form a flocculate which settles out to form a deposit.

Gelatin, Fish See Isinglass.

Glass A translucent, non-reactive substance which is ideally suited to winemaking, since it has no taints to confer on a wine (so long as it is clean).

Glass, Maturing in Unlike wood, glass has no pores in it to allow access of oxygen to the maturing wine. The only oxygen it receives is in minute amounts through the cork, and at racking times when it receives such large quantities as to be in danger of over-oxidation. However, despite this, for the average amateur, glassware is still the best material, if not wishing to become involved in cooperage. But, extra time will be required for optimum oxidative changes, by comparison with casks.

Glasses Whatever may be said, there is only one glass suitable for drinking wine—one large enough to hold a reasonable quantity, with a slight tulip shape so that the bouquet does not escape to the atmosphere. There are designs for glasses for every type of wine, which are impressive but not essential. For the one glass person, it is hard to beat the tulip tasting glass.

Glaze The surface of earthenware vessels are covered with decorative and waterproofing compounds before being baked or fired. Until recently, many of these glazes were based on lead compounds—a dangerous practice for the winemaker, since lead is leached into acid liquids. Lead glazes can be recognised by their softness. Any suspect container should be discarded.

Glucose The most important hexose monosaccharide to winemaking. It is a constituent of all the disaccharides encountered in winemaking and in long chains it forms starch, cellulose and dextrins. Once released from its disaccharide, glucose enters the fermentative pathways to yield alcohol. Residual sugar in a wine is usually glucose or fructose.

Glyceric Acid One of the substances produced as a step in the metabolism of sugars. A hexose is broken down to two three-carbon sugars (trioses), which are then changed to glyceric acid or glycerine. The latter remains in the wine unchanged, while the glyceric acid continues in the fermentation pathway.

Glycerine The major by-product of fermentation. It is formed during early fermentation, when it acts as a hydrogen acceptor to co-enzymes until acetaldehyde is produced and takes over that rôle. Once formed, it plays no further part in the chemistry of alcohol production. For some unknown reason it is formed in larger amounts in wines made from botrytised grapes (perhaps the mould contains an enzyme poisonous to acetaldehyde production). The effect of glycerine on the finished wine is to confer a smoothness on it. It can be used to this effect on an over harsh wine, to mask the astringency.

Glycerine of Borax See Borax, Glycerine of.

Glycerol The chemical name for glycerine.

Glycogen All living things store food. Yeasts are like man in that they store it as glycogen, which is composed of long chains of glucose.

Glycolysis The term for the breakdown of sugars to carbon dioxide and water, with the release of energy. To the winemaker, the pathway finishes at the alcohol stage. (See Appendix IX).

Gm The abbreviation for gram

Grain All cereal plants yield grain. They are of limited value in winemaking, since their main use is in giving body to a wine, and bananas or grape concentrate are both far superior. Cereals contain starch and, to prevent hazes from this, amylase must be used. Grains are low in acid so that assay and correction are needed. Also, they are low in nitrogenous salts, so, if nutrients are not used, the resultant wine will be high in fusel oils and hangover potential! Do not believe it when told that cereal wines get stronger after maturing. Once a wine has finished fermenting its alcohol content will not change (unless fortified!).

Grain for Body tend to confer an unpleasant bouquet and taste on a wine, so that it is better to use bananas or grape concentrate instead.

Grain, Preparation of After soaking the grain for 24-48 hours in cold sulphited water, crush it. Then, after blending the must, add enzymes and yeast.

Graisse The French word for Leuconostoc infection.

Gram The metric unit of weight which is defined as the weight of 1 cc of water at 4°C. It is about 1/30th of an ounce. See (Appendix XII).

Granulated Sugar See Sucrose.

Grapes To the amateur winemaker, the grape is merely another ingredient for wines! To the snob, they are the *only* ingredient for wine. It is incontrovertable that grapes as a lone ingredient produce the best wines, but 'country' wines at least as good as lesser vintages can be produced from the garden. Even though the grape does not require blending with other ingredients, it may still in poor years require chaptalisation. On the whole, grapes have sufficient acid, nutrients, sugar and water to produce wines without any additions except for the yeast.

Grape Concentrate There are now many brands of grape juice on the market. Some of these are excellent and produce good wines merely by following the recipe. Others are not so good and, in order to avoid disappointment, it is best to get advice before buying.

Grape Concentrate for Body and Vinosity Most amateur wines will benefit from a few ounces of grape juice per gallon. Depending on the wine style planned, the amount will vary from ¼–1 pint per gallon, the light bodied requiring less, up to the full amounts for clarets, dessert or port type wines.

Grape Juice fermented produces white wine, irrespective of the colour of the grape; indeed, much of the French white wine is made from red grapes. Red wines are obtained by pulp fermentation of red grapes.

Grape Tannin See Tannin.

Gravity is not a true scale of measurement, but is used as an abbreviation of Specific Gravity. It is the amount by which the Specific Gravity is above or below 1·000; i.e. a Specific Gravity of 1010 is a gravity of 10, while a Specific Gravity of 0·996 equals a gravity of −4.

Green Vegetables can be used as a base ingredient. However, acid and nutrients are essential, since these plants are lacking in both.

Green Vegetables, Preparation of Like most vegetables, these require boiling for about half an hour before blending the must. Most vegetable wines require long maturing.

Gums are complex carbohydrate compounds which, if present in a wine, will cause a haze. They are broken down by pectic enzymes.

Gypsum is added to sherry musts to lower the pH to afford protection against infection. In addition, the lower pH, in some way not understood, aids the formation of the flor. About ½–1 oz per gallon is needed.

— H —

Half Cask See Cask, Half.

Hard Fruit such as apples and pears should be juice fermented if possible. Pulping followed by pressing will extract the juice and this can then be blended with the other ingredients. If pressing facilities are not available the sliced fruit can be pulp fermented for a few days, but this method tends to produce inferior wines. In preparing the fruit care is needed to sulphite immediately since they contain the browning enzyme o-polyphenoloxidase.

Harshness A tasting term to denote a wine in which an alcohol taste is predominant.

Haze A misty appearance in a wine.

Haze, Bacterial Any wine which is infected will eventually show a haze due to the sheer numbers of bacteria in it. It is possible to clear such a wine by sulphiting the wine followed by racking, first to kill and then to rid the wine of the bacteria. (See Diagnosis of Faults, Appendix XI).

Haze, Coloured Metallic　Most metal salts, and it is the salts which cause wine hazes, are coloured. Thus any coloured haze in a wine should be suspected of being due to a metal. The metals commonly affecting wines are: iron, lead, zinc and copper. (See entries for each metal; Diagnosis of Faults, Appendix XI).

Haze, Pectin　Most fruits contain some pectin. As pectin is more soluble in hot water the use of boiling techniques are not recommended for fruits. Unless pectic enzymes are used, the pectin, which is not broken down to any extent by yeast, will form a haze. (See Diagnosis of Faults, Appendix XI).

Haze, Starch　Since starch is not metabolised by yeast enzymes, any cereal or potato in a wine will need amylase added to prevent a starch haze. (See Test for Starch).

Haze, Yeast　After a wine has apparently finished fermenting, it may in fact still be active. As this depends on live yeast in the wine, there may be, depending on the size of the colony, a haze. To remove this, the yeast must be inhibited or killed by either cooling or sulphiting. (See Diagnosis of Faults, Appendix XI).

Heat, Colour Extraction by　While a reasonable technique for preparing grape concentrates, it is not recommended for must preparation, since the use of heat is likely to confer a cooked taste on the wine. The exception to this is in the preparation of vegetables.

Heat for Sterilising　Do not heat sterilise plastics—most of them melt at high temperatures! If using this technique for glassware, there are two possible methods. Either using a pressure cooker with a small amount of water and placing the equipment on the perforated plate. The combination of heat and pressure is akin to the conditions used in autoclaving. This method is limited by the size of the pan. The other method is to bake equipment in the oven at a temperature of 150°C (300°F, gas mark 2) for one hour. Whichever method is used, it is vital to use protective gloves against burns.

Heater, Immersion　See Immersion Heater.

Herbs in Wine For table wines it is best to avoid the use of herbs, since their strong flavour may overpower the taste of the food. On the other hand, many aperitifs *are* herb flavoured wines, Dubonnet and Cinzano for example.

Herbs, Preparation of Pour boiling water over the herbs (dried or fresh) to sterilise them and, after blending with the must, extract sufficient flavour by pulp fermentation.

Hexokinase Once sugar has been broken down to glucose and fructose, the glucose is then split into two molecules of trioses by this enzyme.

Hexose Any sugar containing six carbon atoms in its structure, ie glucose and fructose.

Higher Alcohols See Amyl Alcohol; Fusel Oil.

Honey is the basic ingredient of mead. It is the form in which bees store foodstuff, obtained from the pollens of flowers. Since it is high in bacterial contamination, it is essential to ensure sterility by boiling or, preferably, with sulphite.

Hydrocarbon A compound composed of hydrogen and carbon. None of these compounds are involved in winemaking as such, but some of them (benzene and the phenols) form the basis of tannins and plant pigments.

Hydrogen The simplest element known to man. It plays an important rôle in winemaking from being a component of alcohol and water to rôles in pH and acidity.

Hydrogen Ion When hydrogen enters solution it undergoes a change known as ionisation as a result of which it becomes acidic. By measuring the concentration of hydrogen ions in a solution the pH is obtained.

Hydrogen Ion Concentration See pH.

Hydrogen Peroxide The addition of this reagent to a wine containing iron will cause cloudiness. The reaction may take 24 hours.

Hydrogen and Reduction See Reduction.

Hydrogen Sulphide The once smelled never to be forgotten stink of rotten eggs. If a wine is racked and sulphited to stop fermentation early, the yeast may reduce the sulphur dioxide to hydrogen sulphide. The other cause of this off aroma is the use of sulphur wicks to sterilise barrels. The sulphur may drip on to the wood, impregnate it and then undergo the same reduction. If such a smell is noticed, the cure is to *add* 100 ppm sulphite at about monthly intervals until the smell disappears. The mechanism of this cure is the formation and precipitation of sulphur from the interaction of hydrogen sulphide and sulphur dioxide.

Hydrolysis A chemical reaction wherein the elements of water are added to a compound. It usually requires an enzyme to catalyse the reaction.

Hydrometer The single most important piece of equipment required by the winemaker. It is an easy instrument to use and understand. Firstly it is labelled with a scale on which 1000 is the reading obtained when floated in pure water. If sugar is added to the water it becomes 'thicker' and so the hydrometer does not sink as far as the 1000 mark. Thus a must may have an initial gravity of 1100. After fermentation is complete, the reading may be below 1000. This is because alcohol is lighter than water and, if all the sugar added to the must is converted to alcohol, the gravity may be less than 1000. By using the hydrometer when preparing the must and when testing the finished wine, it is possible to work out the alcohol content of the wine. Also, it can be used to time the stopping of fermentation when making a sweet wine. If the final gravity is: 998 or less, wine is dry;

  998–1005, wine is medium;

  1005–1030, wine is sweet;

  1030 or more, stuck ferment. (See Dry Wine; Sweetness).

Hydrometer and Alcohol Measurement Most winemaking hydrometers have a potential alcohol scale on them. This is useful to the beginner but not quite accurate since these scales presume that fermentation continues to dryness and are not usually corrected for the presence of insolubles in the wine or must.

Hydrometer Errors If the temperature is not that marked on the instrument the reading will have to be corrected according to the table in Appendix VII. The other common cause of error is not reading the scale correctly. The true S.G. is taken at the level of the liquid and not the height to which it rises by surface tension.

Hydrometer, Use of Fruit juices after pressing should have their S.G. measured to assess the natural sugar content. (36 units on the scale equals one pound of cane sugar.) From this the amount required to reach the starting gravity can be calculated.

Hygiene See Cleaning; Sterilizing.

Hypochlorite A chemical which releases chlorine when mixed with water. If using this sterilising agent be careful to choose a non-scented product such as the baby-bottling sterilising solutions. Be sure to thoroughly rinse equipment after sterilising with chlorine as it is an inhibitor of yeast, as well as being unpleasant tasting.

— **I** —

Immersion Heater The type used for tropical fish tanks with a thermostat is a useful piece of equipment to keep the fermentation at the correct temperature in winter. Care must be taken to ensure that it will switch off at 70°F (21°C), to prevent killing the yeast. The other possible trouble with immersion heaters is that sugar in the wine may become caramelised.

Indicator A chemical compound which alters colour with a change in pH. By using one which changes colour at the neutral pH of 7, acidity measurement can be accurately performed.

Indicator Paper Modern indicator papers no longer 'indicate' merely acidity or alkalinity, but by colourimetric scale show the pH. These are available on rolls which cover all or part of the pH scale. For the winemaker, narrow range papers covering the range from 1–4 and 4–6 will be found to be adequate. A drop of wine is placed on a piece of the paper and, after developing the colour, the pH is read off the scale.

Infection can be said to occur in a wine if an unwanted or harmful micro-organism gains access to the wine. (See Bacteria entries; Diagnosis of Faults, Appendix XI).

Infection, Defences against See Acidity, Role of; Alcohol and Sterilisation; Cleaning; Sulphite; Sterilisation.

Infusion The soaking of ingredients in a medium known to dissolve the required flavours, colour, etc. The making of many liqueurs and aperitifs requires the extraction of substances soluble only in alcohol or in water at temperatures which would volatilise them. Obviously, infusion in an alcohol solution (ie wine) is the method to use!

Ingredient Any vegetable, fruit, leaf or flower known to be non-poisonous is acceptable as an ingredient. To these basic ingredients must be added sugar, acids, additives and yeast.

Ingredient, Blending The purpose in blending is to attempt to improve on shortcomings in ingredients. For example, flowers on their own make thin wines, so that blending with an ingredient known to give a good body will improve the finished wine. Since nearly all commercial wines are blended at some time in their lives, there can be no stigma attached in blending country wine.

Inhibition of Fermentation See Citrus Peel and Inhibition; Fermentation, Inhibitors.

Innoculation The addition of yeast to a must.

Inorganic Constituents of Wine See Metals; Salts; Sulphur; Water.

Insensible Fermentation A poor term used sometimes to describe maturation. Since it could logically be taken to mean the later stages of fermentation, which can indeed be almost insensible to the observer, its use should be avoided.

Insipidity A tasting term used to describe a wine lacking in character. It is usually due to a lack of acid or tannin.

Inversion of Sugar The first stage in the utilisation of sucrose by yeast is the splitting of the disaccharide into two monosaccharides. This is accomplished by the enzyme *invertase*. If desired, inversion can be achieved by boiling the sugar in water to which a small amount of acid, citric or tartaric, has been added. This is not a necessary step to take since any wine yeast is capable of inverting sucrose.

Invert Sugar See Sugar, Invert.

Iodine is used in winemaking to test for a starch haze. The addition of a few drops of iodine solution to 5–6 mls of wine will result in a purple colour if starch is present. A brown colour is merely the colour of the iodine.

Ionisation When an atom dissociates in solution it becomes ionised and each atom or radical becomes electrically charged. If hydrogen ions predominate the solution is acid; if hydroxyl ions, it is alkaline.

Iron need never come into contact with wine. If it does, it will cause a haze difficult or even impossible to remove. If present, it is usually due to the use of chipped or cracked enamel ware. The haze may be coloured with a blue tinge or it may be white.

Iron, Tests for (a) Add a few drops of sulphite. The formation of a yellow precipitate indicates a possible iron haze. (b) The formation of a turbitity within 24 hours of adding hydrogen peroxide means that a wine may develop an iron haze. (c) Quantan (cf).

Iron Haze Removal 5 per cent citric acid in 10 per cent sulphite solution, or 5 per cent tannic acid solution, may clear the wine. A trial fining is required before scale treatment. If this fails, it is best to discard the wine.

Isinglass Prepared from the swim bladder of the sturgeon, it is also known as fish gelatin. It is difficult to prepare for use and so its use as a fining agent has been superseded by gelatin.

Iso-electric Point Proteins have the peculiar property of being able to exist as either acids or alkalis, depending on the pH of their solution. Midway between being acid and alkali (the iso-electric point) they are neither and instead, tend to be denatured, and precipitate out of solution. During maturation as acids are esterified the pH of the wine alters and if it nears the iso-electric point of a protein clearing will occur. If, however, the pH alters away from the iso-electric point a colloidal suspension may be formed, perhaps causing a haze.

Isomer Organic compounds are three-dimensional structures. Because of this, arrangement of their atoms in the molecule can vary, although the chemical formula remains the same. For a simple analogy to an isomer look in the mirror, while examining a recent photograph, and note the differences.

— J —

Jar The commonly used term for a gallon sized container. (U.S.A.—jug).

Jelly Bag A stout bag, usually cone shaped, for filtering pulp. It is best to use synthetic fibre such as nylon for strength, ease of cleaning and non-tainting properties.

Jelly Fining See Gelatine.

Judging The appreciation of wines in competitions as laid down by the rules.

Juice The liquid obtained by crushing fruit.

Jug The American equivalent of the demi-john. Similarly, it has an ear handle and a capacity of 1 gallon, (U.S.)

Juice, Adjusting In order to obtain a balanced must, analysis is important. After assay, the necessary corrections can be made to the acidity, sugar, S.G. and pH.

Juice Extraction See Extraction of Juice.

Juice Extractors See Extractors.

Juice Fermentation See Fermentation, Juice.

— K —

Ketone Chemical compounds present only in trace amounts as a by-product of fermentation. They do, however, play an important part in the bouquet of the wine.

Ketose A sugar containing a carbonyl group. The common one to winemakers is fructose.

Kloeckera One of the commonest of the apiculate yeasts.

— L —

Label Apart from the decoration, labels can and do give a great deal of information to the drinker. Most amateurs content themselves with a label merely stating the wine type, although there are elaborate labels available. Even though the label can cost half as much as the wine, the cost is justified in the enhancement of the presentation.

Labelling The label should be placed midway between the seams of the bottle. It should be straight, and no glue visible. For competitions, the rules governing the labelling of entries should be followed.

Lactase The enzyme which splits lactose into its component molecules of glucose and galactose. As wine yeasts do not secrete this enzyme, lactose is a good non-fermentable sweetening agent.

Lactic Acid is a by-product of fermentation and is, therefore, present in trace amounts in a wine. It is produced in large amounts when a wine is infected by lactobacilli. Unlike many of the by-products or off-flavours, it is not toxic. (See Malo-Lactic Reaction.)

Lactobacillus Bacteria which, depending on which species infects a wine, can be considered as either spoilage or beneficial. (See Bacteria, Lactic Acid *et seq.*)

Lactobacillus Haze See Diagnosis of Faults, Appendix XI.

Lactose is the main sugar found in milk. It is a hexose disaccharide, which is broken down to glucose and galactose by the enzyme lactase. Since yeasts do not secrete this enzyme, lactose is non-fermentable. Lactose can, therefore, be used as a sweetening agent, despite it being only one-third as sweet as sucrose.

Laevulose The old name for fructose, so given because of its property of rotating polarised light to the left.

Lag Phase See Fermentation, Lag Phase.

Law As applied to amateur winemaking is basically simple. Make as much as you like; drink as much as you like BUT *do not sell any*. It is illegal to give wine to a charity such as bring and buy sales. Do not distil or fractionate your wines, but only fortify them with duty paid spirit. Penalties for infringements are rightly heavy. Apart from the financial loss, the equipment and alcohol is impounded too. (See Duty; Distillation; Fortification; Fractionating).

Laying down The term used to describe the storing of wines for the period of their final maturation in the bottle. The word no doubt derives from the practice of placing the bottles on their sides, to prevent the drying of the corks.

Lead A toxic soft metal which is gradually being phased out of everyday use (ie from paints, crayons, water pipes and toys). It is to be hoped that the winemaker is doing the same by no longer using the soft glazed pots they may still possess. Lead is not a poison which produces rapid obvious ill-effects, but instead it is gradually stored up in the body until the sufferer is seriously ill. Look for blue lines round the gums if you suspect lead poisoning. Other effects are abdominal pains, weakness and pallor.

Lead Acetate A chemical which can be used to show the presence of hydrogen sulphide. If used, it must not be added to the wine, as it is toxic. The best method of use is to prepare lead acetate paper and place that in the stream of gas coming off from the wine.

Lead Glaze See Glaze.

Lead Poisoning is an insidious disease which very often is not apparent until late in the illness. This is because lead is an accumulative poison, ie the body has difficulty in getting rid of it and, instead, stores it up. Often the first sign of the poisoning is the blue-black lines that appear around the gum margins. Like many other illnesses, prevention is easier than the cure. Do not put wine into any container made with lead.

Leaf Wines Any non-poisonous leaf is a possible base ingredient for a wine. The amount of leaves required is usually of the order of 1 gallon of leaves per gallon of wine. Preparation is by pouring boiling water over them to kill the insect population. It is important with making leaf wines to add sufficient nutrients and acid, since both these groups of additives are lacking.

Lees The sediment at the bottom of the jar or bottle. At the end of fermentation it is composed mostly of yeast débris and insoluble salts. If present in the bottle, it is, or should be, tannins precipitating out of a red wine. A white wine should have no sediment in the bottle.

Lemon Juice An expensive way of using citric acid. The juice from one lemon is equal to about 7 grams of citric acid. This works out at about 5 times the cost of citric acid! The other drawback to its use is not knowing exactly how much acid has been added.

Leuconostoc One of the species of lactobacilli.

Licence No licence is required now to make beer or wine. BUT one is needed before selling alcohol, or distilling or rectifying spirits.

Life of Wine Home-made wines, if properly made, should have a cellar life as good as an equivalent commercial product.

Once opened, however, the commercials 'go off' quicker than the home-made. So far, no explanation has been given for this, except possibly that it may be due to a greater alcoholic strength in home-made wines.

Light See Actinic Action of Sunlight.

Linen Closet (American) See airing cupboard.

Liqueur A strongly alcoholic drink made from distilled spirits with some form of additional flavouring—herbs, spices, honey, etc. They are usually drunk after dinner. With the range of essences available, the amateur can produce his own. Be warned, the cost of the fortifying spirit is about 90 per cent of the cost.

Litmus The use of litmus paper is now receding in favour of pH papers which can give results accurate to about half a unit. Litmus paper is of value only to determine if a solution is acid or alkaline. (See Indicator Paper.)

Loaf Sugar An expensive way of buying sugar. How boring it must be trying to dissolve it!

Lock, Fermentation See Air-Lock.

Longevity of Wine is dependent on several factors. The greater the alcohol content, the greater the life. Tannin plays an important part in wine life, for red wines have a longer life than white ones. A good cork and capsule on a bottle stored in the proper way at the correct temperature is the final step in keeping a wine of quality at its peak. (See Life of Wine).

— **M** —

Madeira A generic name given to wines which are heated prior to maturation. The heating processes cause caramelisation of the residual sugar. (See Estufagem.)

Maderisation See Caramelisation.

Magnesium A metal necessary for some chemical reactions.

In hard water areas enough is present in tap water for winemaking. In soft water areas about 0.5 gms per gallon are required.

Magnesium Sulphate The soluble form of magnesium which is the usual source of magnesium in winemaking.

Malic Acid The principal acid in apples, whence it gets its name. This is one of the main acids in grapes, being especially prevalent in the unripe fruit. As ripening occurs the malic acid content falls. In some of the northern vineyards the malic acid level never falls greatly, so that the malo-lactic reaction is encouraged. Malic acid is a bitter acid and if predominant will produce a sharp wine. Its use is chiefly in esterification.

Malo-Lactic Bacteria See Bacteria, Lactic Acid.

Malo-Lactic Fermentation See another term for Malo-lactic reaction.

Malo-Lactic Reaction A lacto-bacillus infection of wine which results in malic acid being broken down to lactic acid. The acidity of the wine is lowered as well as the acid taste, since lactic acid tastes less acid than malic.

Malo-Lactic Reaction and Bottle Fermentation Sometimes the malo-lactic fermentation occurs after bottling. If it is discovered, the wine should be put back under air-lock to prevent explosions. If a pétillant wine is wanted, then the wine should be racked into clean (non-sulphited) champagne bottles where there is no danger of the pressure breaking the bottles.

Malo-Lactic Reaction, Conditions for A young wine which has a high malic acid content is the first requirement. It must not have been filtered or sulphited (the bacteria will be removed by such a process), and the wine should be dry. Any residual sugar will be broken down to the bitter sugar mannitol. There is no known way of encouraging this infection and, commercially, an active malo-lactic fermentation is added as a starter to a young wine.

Malt Barley, after partial germination and kilning, is known as malt. It is used in some recipes, but its main use to the winemaker is as the dried extract for preparing starters.

Maltose The principal sugar of barley which is only slowly fermented by wine yeasts.

Mannitic Infection occurs in stuck ferments at high temperatures. The bacteria (one of the lacto-bacilli) breaks down fructose to mannitol. Prevention is by ensuring sufficient acid in a well prepared must and protecting against infection. There is no cure for this condition and it is best to discard the wine, should it occur.

Mannitol A sugar with a bitter taste produced by one of the lacto-bacilli. If a sweet wine undergoes a malo-lactic fermentation, there is a chance that mannitol will be formed.

Mannose A sugar which is commonly found as a constituent of plant protein. It is fermented by wine yeasts.

Marc The French word for pulp after it has been pressed. (See Brandy.)

Marriage During maturation the constituents of the embryonic wine interact, so that when it is ready for drinking, all the components harmonize with each other. This process is somewhat poetically called the marriage.

Maturation The complex processes a wine goes through from the end of fermentation, when it probably tastes foul, to the time of drinking, when it should be superb! It embraces bottling, casking, cellarcraft and racking.

Maturation and Acidity Apart from the bacteriocidal effect of a correct acidity, the proper acid balance will benefit the wine during maturation as the succinic and malic acids esterify to form compounds which will eventually aid the bouquet. A wine which is low in acid will not improve. Instead it may develop a medicinal taste. An over-acid wine will mellow during maturation and although a lot of time is needed it should eventually become drinkable.

Maturation in Bottle See Bottle Maturing.

Maturation in Bulk A wine matured in small casks will

mature faster than in large ones. This is because the volume/surface-area ratio dictates the amount of oxygen that can be absorbed by the wine for oxidation reactions. Ideally maturing should be a slow process to allow reactions to occur and the old and new compounds to blend together. Thus a cask with a large volume will supply less oxygen and the process will take longer. For the amateur, the counsel of perfection is difficult to achieve, since not many possess the space to mature wine in commercial sized casks!

Maturation in Cask See Cask Maturing.

Maturation, Chemistry of During this time malic and succinic acids are esterified; fusel oils broken down to acids and aldehydes; small amounts of acetic acid formed; and aldehydes and alcohol join to form acetals.

Maturation, Conditions required The bottle cellar is ideal for maturing, provided that it is dark and dry and cool.

Maturation and Esterification A long, slow process which involves the joining of acids and alcohols to form compounds which play a large part in flavour and bouquet. The acids required for esterification are malic and succinic. The latter is a by-product of fermentation, but its addition in small amounts will certainly aid the process. Ester formation takes place largely after bottling (it is a reduction process) and it is to encourage this reaction that quality wines should be allowed a year or so in bottle before tasting.

Maturation in Glass Provided the wine receives oxygen by, firstly, a cork bung (although the amount is small it is significant), and, secondly, by regular rackings, it will mature satisfactorily. The end result will not be as good as with cask maturing but it will be quite acceptable. The possible reason for this is that the wine matures at an uneven rate, unlike the slow constant rate in cask.

Maturation and Oxidation See Oxidation and Maturing.

Maturation and Reduction See Reduction.

Maturation and Tannin During maturation, the tannin content of a red wine falls. Some is oxidised; some joins with protein and other constituents in the wine; and some will precipitate out of the wine. The overall effect of this will be the lessening of the astringency and, since the tannin content takes a long time to fall to a palatable level, a better quality wine, due to a longer period for other constituents to marry with each other.

Maturation Temperature should ideally be about 55°F (10°C). Warmer than this will mean that chemical reactions, which go faster at a higher temperature, will progress too fast, with the result that the wine will mature too quickly for quality.

Maturation, Time required White wines mature fairly fast, as they are not protected from over-oxidation as are reds. This must be borne in mind when casking a white wine. For the amateur, 2–3 months in a 4-gallon barrel is all that a white wine will stand without becoming over-oxidised. Red wines, on the other hand, may withstand the same conditions for 2–3 years. The point is that there are no rules as to time. The end of casking is gauged on taste—when a wine tastes almost drinkable, bottle it.

Mead Derived from a Greek word meaning wine, it has come to mean a drink made from fermented honey. Its relatives, such as metheglin (spiced mead) and melomel (fruit and honey) are not accepted as mead by the purists.

Measures For winemaking, it is necessary to be able to measure weight to an ounce accurately (less than this should be performed with solutions or beam balances). Volume measurement requires 100 ml calibrated jars, pint jugs and a 1 gallon calibrated jar. Most of these can be borrowed from the kitchen. (See Appendix XII for weight and measure conversion charts).

Méchage The French word for burning sulphur wicks in barrels.

Medium Not the genie who predicts the quality of future vintages, but a solution or jelly for growing yeasts! A medium must contain foodstuffs, nutrients and vitamins and must be sterile.

Medicinal Taste An off-flavour, variously described, which once tasted is never to be forgotten. It is due to a lack of acid in the must. Prevention is by acid control in the must. A cure may be possible by sweetening, but the safest treatment is discarding the wine.

Melomel A wine made with fruit juice and honey.

Meniscus All liquids have a *surface tension* which is the property which keeps them liquid. Without this, they would become gases. The effect of this is to cause the liquid to rise or fall slightly where it meets the walls of a container. It is important to ignore the meniscus in SG measurement. The SG is taken at the point where the main level of the liquid lies and not at the top of the meniscus. Failure to appreciate this may give rise to an error of 5–6 in the gravity.

Meso-Inisitol A compound which is not a true sugar, although it has a similar structure. It is an important vitamin to the yeast and the use of malt in the starter will supply sufficient.

Metabisulphite The chemical radical from which campden tablets are made and which is the storage form of sulphur dioxide, the active sterilising agent. When placed in water it is broken down to bisulphite which then liberates sulphur dioxide gas. The word is usually abbreviated to sulphite or bisulphite. The subject is fully discussed under the former headings.

Metabisulphite, Sodium and Potassium The commercially available preparations of sulphite are sold in powder form as the sodium or potassium salts, or as Campden tablets.

Metabolism The term given to the series of chemical reactions in which foodstuffs are broken down to yield energy and waste products.

Metal Chemical elements which are characterised by so many variables that no accurate definition can be given. Many of them play an important part in yeast metabolism as cofactors. Some metals, notably lead, are toxic and should not be allowed near a wine.

Metallic Casse A haze due to metallic compounds entering solution in a wine.

Metal, Fining of is possible to the professional using EDTA (ethylene diamine tetra-acetate). This method is safer than the one involving the use of ferrocyanide, which is a deadly poison. For the amateur it is sometimes possible to effect a degree of cure with the use of 5% citric acid. (See Iron Haze Removal).

Metal Haze See Casse, Metallic.

Metallic Taste A descriptive term for the distinctive off-flavour due to metal contamination. A wine so affected does have a definite taste of metal.

Metal, Dangerous Do not use toxic metals such as lead and brass. Non-toxic but haze causing metals such as copper and iron should also be avoided.

Metheglin Spiced mead. The word is derived from the Welsh word meaning *medicine*.

Methyl Alcohol See Alcohol, Methyl.

Meths A fuel composed of ethyl and methyl alcohols and a foul smelling substance, pyridine. Despite its toxicity, it is still drunk by some addicts. It is used in winemaking as a test solution for the presence of pectin. (See Alcohol, Methyl).

Mg or mgm The abbreviations for milligram (one-thousandth of a gram).

Micro-Organism Any unicellular plant or animal which cannot be seen by the naked eye. They have a wide range of functions. For the winemaker, two classes of importance are the yeasts and the bacteria.

Mildew   An infection of plants which, if it affects grapes, will ruin the crop. (See Botrytis Cinerea; Mould).

Milk   A very simple but effective fining agent. A few drops per gallon are all that are usually required. The amount can be determined by trial fining. It is easier to use than casein, (which is the active fining agent present in milk).

Milton   A commercial sterilising agent based on hypochlorite.

Mineral   Any inorganic salt or metal. They are of importance to yeast reproduction and metabolism as vitamins, catalysts or co-factors. (See Calcium; Magnesium; Phosphates; Potassium; Sulphite).

Mixture of Acids   The discussion goes on and will go on for a long time yet as to the best formulation to use for acid addition. Some authorities consider citric acid alone to be adequate; others that mixtures of the acids give better results. The ratios of acid suggested vary, dependent on the fruit acid present.

Mixture, Freezing   See Freezing Mixture.

Moeslinger Fining   Another name for the highly poisonous potassium ferricyanide.

Monobasic   The term used to describe an acid which has one hydrogen ion available on dissociation.

Monosaccharide   A one-unit sugar.

Mother of Vinegar   Another name for mycoderma aceti.

Mould   Members of the plant kingdom related to the yeasts, which cause infections in wines. Some people consider they confer an improvement on a wine. To most, however, the taste of damp rot is not what they want in their wine! (See Botrytis Cinerea; Mildew).

Mousiness The after taste caused by acetoin, a metabolite of one of the lactobacilli. Prevention is by hygiene. Cure is not possible; the wine must be discarded. (See Acetamide).

Mousseux The term which, by French law, has to be put on the label of a French sparkling wine not made in Champagne.

Muselet The French word for the wire ties used on Champagne bottles.

Must To the beginner, a schizophrenic word! To the winemaker, it is not the emphasising of an order; it is the prepared juice, from the time of its preparation until the end of fermentation, when it may then be called (if not considered!) wine. The word is derived from the Latin word *mustus* meaning new.

Mycelium The long branching chains in which moulds grow. It is also their chief anatomical characteristic.

Mycoderma Aceti Another name for acetobacter.

Mycoderma Vini Another name for candida mycoderma.

— **N** —

Natural Sugar The sugar present in the base ingredients. To determine its value, extract the juice and take the SG. Deduct 7 to allow for the solids in the juice. From this can be calculated the sugar addition required. The only fruit which have a high enough natural sugar content to make wine consistently are grapes.

Natural Yeast See Bloom of Fruit.

Neutral Spirit A term for a colourless, tasteless (except for the alcohol) spirit, such as Vodka, useful for fortification purposes.

Nitrate The naturally occurring salts from which plants obtain their nitrogen. Yeasts cannot utilise these salts and so, despite plenty of nitrogen in a must, more has to be added in a form the yeast can metabolise. (See Additives; Ammonium phosphate; Nitrogen).

Nitrogen One of the most important elements in the cell structure. All proteins contain nitrogen. Plants build up their protein from the soil, a thing other life forms cannot do. Instead, they have to utilise plant protein and rebuild it to suit themselves; ('all flesh is as grass' *is* true). Yeasts require protein and they either obtain it from their dead 'cell mates' (with consequential fusel oil production), or they can build it from ammonium salts.

Noble Mould; Noble Rot English translations of 'Pourriture noble'. (See Botrytis Cinerea).

Non-Vintage Wines such as Port and Champagne do not always bear a year label on the bottle. For this to happen, the wine must be of outstanding quality. Such years as are not declared a vintage are known as non-vintage.

Normal Solution Chemicals are mixed in solutions whose concentration is related to the molecular weight of that particular compound. A normal solution contains the molecular weight in grams per litre of solution. ie Sodium hydroxide has a molecular weight of 40, so that a normal solution will contain 40 gms per litre of the salt.

Nose Another word for bouquet of a wine.

Nutrient See Additive; Nitrogen.

Nutrient Salt See Ammonium phosphate; Magnesium sulphate; Potassium phosphate; Vitamin B.

— O —

Oak Container See Cask entries.

Off-Flavour Any taste in a wine which, as a result of infection or poor fermentative technique destroys the true flavour of the wine. (See Diagnosis of Faults, Appendix XI).

Oil, Fusel See Amyl Alcohol; Fusel Oil.

Oiliness See Diagnosis; Lactobacilli and Ropiness.

O-Polyphenoloxidase See Casse, oxidative; Enzyme, oxidative, Pectic Enzymes and Darkening.

Organic Constituents of Wine See Composition of Wine.

Organism Correctly speaking, means any life form, but bacteriologically it is taken only to include single-celled life forces.

Original Gravity The SG of the must before fermentation is begun. If exponential feeding is practised, it is the SG that the must would have had, had all the sugar been included at the start.

Osmosis One of the laws of nature is that substances in solution pass from a region of high concentration to one of low concentration until they mix fully. For example, a spoonful of sugar placed in a tumbler of water, unstirred, will gradually dissolve. If a barrier is placed between substances which can only let water (or equally small molecules) through, the law has to be observed in a different way. Since they cannot mix, the water has to pass through the barrier to dilute the sugar. If too much sugar is added to a must, this situation applies. Water leaves the yeast to dilute the solution, eventually killing the cells. This results in a stuck ferment. To avoid such a situation, exponential feeding is recommended.

Over-Acid See Acid Reduction.

Over-Fining See Fining.

Over-Pressing Care must be taken not to try to wring out the last drop of juice when pressing. To do so will result in excess tannin entering the must, which in turn will lead to an over astringent harsh wine.

Over-Sweet A wine which stops fermenting too soon, or one which has too much sweetening added will taste syrupy. Even with extra acid added to try to counteract this, the wine will still be cloying. To prevent this, careful fermentation is required and, when sweetening a wine, care must be taken to work out exactly the amount of sugar needed.

Ox Blood See Blood.

Oxalic Acid is present in rhubarb and, since it is toxic, care must be taken with the preparation of this fruit. There is no need, unless the acidity of the juice is too high, to lower the acidity routinely and then add further acid. Provided it is not pressed and *the leaves are not used*, the acidity is usually within acceptable levels. Contrary to the belief of many people, oxalic acid is not the principle acid of rhubarb stalks; malic acid is.

Oxidation Pasteur was the first person to prove the need for oxygen in the ageing of wines. Its function is to react with many of the compounds in the wine and alter them so that they precipitate out, or change them so that they help the wine to become mellow.

Oxidation in Cask See Cask, oxidation in.

Oxidation due to Enzymes See Casse, Oxidative.

Oxidation and Filtration As with any procedure carried out in the presence of air, there is the risk of oxidation. To prevent this, the wine should be sulphited and open funnels should not be used. Rather, use one of the closed systems such as the Vinamat, Boots, Harris or Southern Vinyards filters.

Oxidation and Maturing Some ethyl alcohol is oxidised to acetaldehyde or acetic acid (both of which play important parts in the final flavour of the wine). The higher alcohols are oxidised to aldehydes and, apart from rendering the wine non-toxic, these aldehydes form acetals by combining with alcohol. Some of the tannins are also oxidised.

Oxidation, Prevention of If all procedures involving the transfer of wine from one container to another are carried out as gently as possible to avoid splashing, the oxygen uptake will be kept to a minimum. It is possible to create an oxygen-free atmosphere by piping carbon dioxide from an active ferment into the receiving jar. Other than this, the only methods open to the amateur are the uses of sulphite or ascorbic acid.

Oxidation and Sulphite See Sulphite and Anti-Oxidation.

Oxidation/Reduction Reaction See Redox.

Oxidative Casse See Casse, Oxidative.

Oxidative Enzymes See Enzymes, Oxidative; O-Polyphenoloxidase.

Oxido-Reductase The enzyme which catalyses the reaction to change three carbon sugars to glycerol.

Oxygen is required to encourage a yeast colony to develop after pitching, during the aerobic phase of fermentation. After this, no oxygen is needed until the small amounts required for maturation. During fermentation, oxygen must be excluded to avoid aerobic infection.

— P —

Palate The complex organs which combine together to analyse taste are the palate, nose-mouth and brain. The nose 'tastes' the volatile elements of the flavour, while the mouth and palate analyse the liquid part. It is interesting to note that with the nose occluded (as with a cold), taste is an almost useless function.

Paper, Filter See Filter Paper.

Paper, Litmus See Litmus.

Paper, Indicator See Indicator Paper.

Parts per Thousand Acid analysis of a wine is expressed as *parts per thousand* of sulphuric acid.

Pasteur The French scientist who proved the need for oxygen in the ageing of wines. He also proved the existence of acetobacter by showing that a wine kept sealed or which only received filtered air did not become infected, while a wine left open rapidly became infected. From this he disproved the theory of spontaneous generation of life.

Pasteurisation The heating of liquids to a temperature of 140°F for 3-4 minutes. This has the effect of killing nearly all bacteria and coagulating proteins. If this is practised with wines it has the effect of stopping maturation as the enzymes involved are all denatured (or destroyed).

Pearson Square The equation for working out spirit additions for fortification. (See Fortification Calculation).

Pectic Enzymes and Darkening If enzymes are added prior to pulping, there is a chance that oxidative changes may occur due to the liberation of o-polyphenoloxidase. To prevent this, anaerobic conditions are required, together with sulphiting of the prepared fruit.

Pectin Enzymes and Extraction By breaking down the pectin in the fruit cell wall greater yields of juice can be obtained. If heating techniques have been used allow the juice to cool before adding the enzymes, to avoid denaturing.

Pectic Enzymes and Tannin A red wine with a pectin haze will tend to clear better than a white wine, because the latter has almost no tannin. This group of acids being oppositely charged to many of the colloidal hazes will help to clear a wine so afflicted by neutralising the charge on the haze-causing pectin.

Pectin is a complex substance which forms part of the cell wall in plants. It is composed of long chains of galactonuric acid whose side chains of methyl alcohol are the chief source of the trace amounts of methanol found in all wines.

Pectin, Action of In nature pectin is one of the main structural components of plant cell walls. If extracted into solution, it will tend to 'gel' (which is hoped for in the making of jams). When present in a wine, it is not (or should not be), in such a concentration as to produce a jelly. It will, however, cause a haze if not broken down during fermentation.

Pectin and Boiling Pectin is more soluble at higher temperatures, which is one of the main reasons for trying to avoid heating ingredients when preparing a must. Also, in heating or boiling a pectin-containing fruit, the natural pectin destroying enzymes are denatured, making the use of pectin enzyme even more imperative.

Pectinase The naturally-occurring enzymes which can break down some of the pectin extracted from fruit during must preparation. If heat is used for this, the enzyme will be denatured. The commercial preparations of pectin-destroying powders or solutions contain the same enzyme.

Pectin-destroying Enzymes *Natural enzymes* are present on fruit containing pectin and these will break down a small amount of pectin extracted in fruit fermentation. However, if the fruit has been heated, the extraction of pectin is greater, and the enzymes denatured so that the addition of commercial preparations of these enzymes is required. It is better to add pectic enzymes before fermentation as a routine than to try to clear a pectin haze.

Pectin Glycoside The active enzyme in 'Rohament P' which breaks down cellulose connective tissue in fruits to increase juice yield. Pectinase must be used with this enzyme to prevent pectin hazes.

Pectin Haze As molecules of pectin have electrical charges, they are one of the causes of colloidal hazes in wines. By adding pectic enzymes, the haze will not necessarily clear, since the electrical charge can be transferred to other particles. If the use of pectinase is not practiced prior to, then it must be used after fermentation, and a period allowed for natural clearing followed by fining.

Pectin Occurrence   Pectin is present in all fruit to some extent. The riper the fruit, the greater the amount. Fruit that are especially high in pectin are apricots, citrus, parsnips, peaches and plums. The North American cherry has a low content.

Pectin Removal   is best done immediately after any extraction method during must preparation. *DO NOT ADD ENZYMES TO A HOT SOLUTION*. It is a good idea to use pectic enzymes routinely when preparing the must rather than trying to clear a pectin haze in a finished wine.

Pectin, Test for   15 ml of methylated spirit added to 5 ml of wine will cause gelling of pectin if present. This is usually visible as small clots forming in the test solution. These may take up to two hours to appear.

Peel and Inhibition   See Citrus Peel and Inhibition.

Pellicle   The skin which forms on the surface of a wine infected by certain of the spoilage bacteria. A sherry flor is the one example of a pellicle which is beneficial to wine.

Penicillium   Species of mould best known as antibiotics which may grow on a wine not kept under anaerobic conditions. They can be recognised by the blue-green or white colour in a 'hairy' growth. Prevention is by hygiene. Cure is possible by removal of the mould, sulphiting and racking, followed by restarting. If the wine is tainted, it should be discarded.

Pentose   One of the main groups of monosaccharides. They are characterised by five carbon atoms in their structure. An example is arabinose. Pentoses are not fermented by wine yeasts.

Peptide Link   The special chemical bond between amino-acids, whereby they join together to form proteins. The bond is between the amine radical of one acid and the carboxyl radical of the next.

Perry   A weakly alcoholic drink made from pears.

pH is defined as $1/\log_{10}[H+]$. This is a simplified method of expressing the acidity or alkalinity of a solution. If this were expressed as the number of hydrogen ions present, the figure would be so large as to defy comprehension. pH is a scale ranging from 1 to 14 (from very acid to very alkaline). The more acid a solution, the lower the pH.

pH and Acidity A wine is a buffer solution. If acid is added, although the acidity will rise, the pH may not alter due to this buffering effect.

pH and Spoilage One of the main applications of pH to winemaking is in the prevention of infection. It is well known that most bacteria cannot reproduce if the pH is below 3·5. At this point yeasts are not inhibited. Thus it is always worth checking that the pH is about 3·5 before pitching the yeasts. A well prepared must usually has a pH of about this value.

pH Measurement The simplest and cheapest method is to use narrow range pH papers. One drop of wine is placed on a strip of paper and after the colour has developed it is compared with the result chart. For winemaking, the paper with a range from 1 to 4 is adequate. For the rich, the pH meter measures the pH by the conductivity of the solution. (See Indicator Paper.)

Phenol The six carbon ring structured compound which forms the basic structure for the tannins.

Phenolphthalein A weak acid which changes colour from colourless to red at about the neutral point (pH 7). It is widely used for titrating weak acids with strong alkalis, such as is performed in winemaking. (See Acidity Determination; Indicator).

Phosphates are the most important radical for the storing of energy and its later release in winemaking reactions. It is, effectively, the fuel for reactions requiring energy. Unlike coal, however, it can be reconstituted. (See Ammonium Phosphate; Energy Transfer; Potassium Phosphate.)

Photochemical Deterioration See Actinic Action of Sunlight.

Phylloxera The aphid which almost destroyed the whole of the European vineyards in the 1870s. The vines now used are hybrids, European varieties grafted on to American root stocks.

Pichia A genus of yeast present in the sherry flor. It is a spoilage organism to a table wine, but it is essential for flavour development in sherries. It does not metabolise sugar to alcohol, but instead to aldehydes.

Pinot One of the most important varieties of red grape.

Pip The seed of fruit. In tannin-containing fruit and berries, the pips have a higher tannin content than the rest of the fruit. In red grapes, the pips may contain up to 50 per cent of the total tannin. If a low tannin wine is wanted, do not press the pips, and if possible exclude them from pulp fermentation.

Pipe The special name given to barrels used for Port.

Pipette An accurately calibrated tube which, when filled to the mark etched upon it, contains a precise volume of solution. For winemaking, a 5 or 10 ml pipette is needed for acidity measurement.

Plant Acid See Acid. Plant

P.O.P. See Gypsum.

Plastering The technique of adding gypsum to a sherry must.

Plastic Barrels Provided of a food grade and not tainted by previous contents, such a container is of value for *short term* storage. Their long term usage has not been assessed. Plastics do not admit air in the same way as wooden casks, so it is likely that they are inferior.

Plastic Closures See Closures, Plastic.

Plastic Container See Container, Plastic.

Plastic, Toxic The yellow plastics contain cadmium, but it has been proved that even with a new bucket the amount of cadmium leached into one litre of wine is below the daily dietary intake. To become poisoned would need a lot of litres daily for a long time!

Poisonous Plants Any plant known to produce edible fruit will produce some kind of wine. Poisonous fruit—poisonous wines. If in doubt, *do not experiment*. It is beyond the scope of this book to give a detailed list of dangerous plants.

Polarisation A phenomenon demonstrated by the sugars. Light is made up of light waves which travel in all planes around a point. If a light is shone through a sugar solution, the light does not pass through the solution in some of the planes, ie it is polarised.

Polish Spirit See Fortification.

Polysaccharide Sugars made up of many sugar molecules. (See Dextrin; Pectin; Starch).

Polythene One of the better plastics to use for winemaking. It is a high density material which does not stain easily, nor does it pick up 'off' flavours.

Polyurethane Varnish is non-reactive and waterproof. It is ideal for covering home-made winemaking equipment. Ensure thorough drying as the solvent can taint a wine.

Pome Fruit A type of fruit in which the edible flesh surrounds a core containing seeds. They include apples, hawthorn, medlar, pear and rowan.

Port A fortified wine made in Portugal from the region around Oporto. Before fermentation is completed, the yeast is inhibited by the addition of brandy so that it remains a sweet wine. It requires long maturing and careful handling due to the crust which forms in the bottle. It is usually a blended wine, unless the quality warrants a vintage being declared.

Positioning Bottles Table wines and port should be stored, (or layed down), on their sides so that the wine keeps the cork moist and swollen to prevent shrinkage and possible infection. Fortified wines are usually stored upright to avoid dissolution of the cork by the high alcohol content.

Potassium An important additive for yeast reproduction and metabolism. It is an important constituent of the structure of cells. Its lack will mean a stuck ferment. It is possible to provide too much of this metal and this may result in a haze due to cream of tartar formation by its combining with tartaric acid.

Potassium Bitartrate See Argol; Bitartrate; Cream of Tartar.

Potassium Ferrocyanide See Blue Fining.

Potassium Hydrogen Tartrate The intermediate compound between the soluble tartaric acid and the insoluble pottasium bitartrate.

Potassium Metabisulphite One of the available forms of metabisulphite.

Potassium Phosphate One of the nutrient salts necessary to provide both potassium and phosphate radicals in a must.

Potassium Sorbate This first-rate inhibitor of fermentation was in August 1974 passed as safe by the Committee on the Safety of Drugs. It is available commercially, and is now a permitted chemical to stop fermentation.
N.B: Sulphite should always be used in conjunction with it since it is *only* an inhibitor and not a sterilising agent to counter bacteria.

Potential Alcohol See Alcohol, Potential.

Pourriture Noble See Botrytis.

ppm The abbreviation for 'parts per million'. It is used for sulphite dosage.

ppt The abbreviation for 'parts per thousand', which is used as the unit of acid measurement.

Precipitate An insoluble compound formed by chemical reaction between two compounds in solution. ie Potassium phosphate and tartaric acid combine to form potassium bitartrate.

Precipitated Chalk See Calcium Carbonate.

Preparation of Bananas Peel and slice the fruit. Boil for ½ hour (with or without the skins, depending on the recipe). Then strain and press lightly. If pulp fermentation were to be used, the fruit would break up into an easily disturbed sediment. As it is, even with this method of preparation, banana containing wines tend to have a large sediment.

Preparation of Flowers, Fruit, Grain, Red Fruit, Rhubarb, Vegetables See respective entries.

Press Although not an essential piece of equipment for the small producer, it is useful to have one when large quantities of fruit have to be processed. Always wrap fruit, after crushing or pulping, in cloth. This will prevent the holes in the press becoming clogged by particles of pulp. Do not apply maximum pressure immediately but, after each run of juice, increase the pressure. This will increase the yield and also not put too great a strain on the press.

Pressure Cooker A sealed pan in which it is possible to build up a considerable pressure, thereby reducing the cooking time. They are also useful for sterilising small pieces of equipment.

Pressure in Sparkling Wines See Champagne Bottles, Pressure in.

Primary Fermentation See Fermentation, Primary.

Proof The alcohol measuring scale. In the United Kingdom, 100% proof equals 57·1% alcohol, while in the U.S.A. 100% proof equals 50% alcohol. On the Continent the Gay Lussac scale is used instead, wherein the percentage alcohol equals the degrees Gay Lussac. (See Appendix V).

Propionic Acid is formed by the breakdown of tartaric acid as a result of an infection known as Tourne. The bitterness in a wine so affected is due to the acid produced. Should this infection occur, the wine must be discarded and the winery thoroughly cleaned. Prevention is by attention to hygiene.

Protective Colloid If a wine contains electrically charged particles, they may give their charge to neutral particles in the wine. These newly charged particles often form a haze which proves difficult to clear. The common example of such a haze is one due to pectin.

Protein Animal cells are composed chiefly of protein. In all matter, vegetable or animal, the nuclei of the cells contain protein. These proteins are the basis of the chromosomes which determine reproductive characteristics.

Protein, Albuminous See Albumin.

Protein, Collagenous See Collagen; Gelatin.

Protein Haze A wine low in tannin (usually white) may have a slight haze due to protein. Bentonite fining is the usual method of treatment.

Protein Stability If adding tannin to a white wine before bottling causes a flocculate, that wine is likely to develop a haze. Should this occur, trial fine with tannin and Bentonite and retest before bottling.

Protein, Test for See Quantan DT.

Pulp, Asbestos; Cellulose; Fermentation; Filtration; Settling See respective entries.

Pulper A machine for crushing fruit to facilitate juice extraction.

Pupitre The 'desk' which the widow Cliquot is said to have invented. It is used in Champagne making to hold the bottles during rémuage.

Pyroligneous Acid The distillate of wood from which is obtained methanol.

Pyruvic Acid The compound two away from alcohol in the fermentative pathway. It is a three-carbon molecule derived from glyceric acid which is oxidised to acetaldehyde—the precurser of alcohol. (See Appendices IX and X.)

— Q —

Quaff Swallow copious draughts from a quaich (q.v.).

Quaich Bowl shaped Scottish drinking vessel with double handles, often made of silver and handsomely engraved.

Quart An imperial quart is a quarter of a gallon, containing 40 fl. oz.; the reputed quart is one-sixth of a gallon or $26\frac{2}{3}$ fl. oz. The U.S. quart, one-quarter of a U.S. gallon, is approximately five-sixths the volume of an imperial quart, and is 32 U.S. oz.

Quarter-Cask A medium-sized cask, so named as the quarter of a pipe. However, the vessel known as a 'quarter-cask' may vary in capacity from 25 to 35 imperial gallons.

Quartern A liquor measure, lit. 'one-quarter' but conventionally now used as $\frac{1}{4}$ of a pint bottle.

Quick-Ageing This seems at first self-contridictory, but all it means is a speeding up of the maturation of alcoholic beverages. For many years scientists, the wine trade, and amateur winemakers have striven continually to try to reduce the time required to mature a wine satisfactorily, and the most popular methods have been the use of Senex (activated charcoal) or ion exchange. Pasteurisation, electric discharge, ozonation, alternate heating and freezing and numerous other processes and devices have also been tried. Whether any process is effective is doubtful for it is still common for less scrupulous merchants to fake the age of brandy by adding vanilla, the age of whisky by adding oak extract and so forth.

— R —

Racking The removal of a wine from its deposit. This can be done either by siphoning or pouring. The latter is not so satisfactory, since there is the chance of including lees with the clear wine. Failure to rack a wine soon after fermentation has ceased will lead to the development of off-flavours from the autolysing yeast.

Racking and Fermentation By racking before the end of fermentation, it is possible to obtain a sweet wine. When performed with care, racking will leave behind all the sediment. As this contains nearly all the yeast, it follows that racking two or three times (with the addition of sulphite) before fermentation is complete will totally destroy the yeast colony.

Racking and Sulphite When making sherry, never add sulphite. Other than that, it is a good practice to use sulphite 100 ppm at the first racking and 50 ppm at successive rackings. This is, firstly, to prevent the re-establishment of a new yeast colony and, secondly, to prevent the wine from becoming oxidised. If a malo-lactic reaction is desired, do not add sulphite after fermentation, or the bacteria, if present, will be inhibited.

Racking, Timing of The first racking should be carried out a few days after fermentation has stopped if a dry wine is wanted. After this, the wine needs regular rackings for up to two years at 3–4 monthly intervals, until the oxidative maturation is finished. For white wines, the oxidative changes take less time, and so racking need only continue for 6–12 months. If a sweet wine is required, the wine should be racked before the end of fermentation. (See Racking and Fermentation.)

Radical A constant combination of chemicals which, when made into a compound (with other chemicals or radicals), confer constant physical properties to a series of compounds (e.g. ketones or aldehydes).

Raisin The dried grape. With the price of dried fruit as it is now, their use will probably be superseded by grape concentrate.

Raisin, White The American name for sultanas.

Raisins for Vinosity Since raisins are dried grapes, it follows that their use in a wine will confer 'vinosity' to that wine.

However, the price has risen so much that grape concentrate is the better ingredient to use.

Raisins, Preparation of Mince and pulp ferment for three to four days to extract the sugar. If a deeply coloured wine is required this may be continued longer.

Recipe The list of ingredients, additives, and the method of preparation and production of a wine.

Recipe, No Yeast Many of the older recipes which have not been brought up to date state that the must should be left exposed to the air to allow fermentation to start. This is a risky technique, as the chances of infection are at least as high as that of producing a wine. Do not follow this part of such recipes but instead use an appropriate yeast.

Record Keeping To obtain repeatability and consistency of results, it is vital to keep records with details of ingredients, technique, costs, tasting notes and suggested improvements. These should ideally be in a permanent form such as a book or card index.

Red Fruit contain tannin in their skins and, although, after pressing, juice fermentation is possible, pulp fermentation is better to obtain maximal sugar extraction as well as tannin and colour.

Redox Reaction is a chemical situation where both reduction (*red-*) and oxidation (*-ox*) are taking place at the same time This occurs during bottle maturation and is most important to final quality.

Reduction is either the removal of oxygen; the addition of hydrogen; or the gaining of an electron by a compound during the course of a chemical reaction. These reactions occur mostly during bottle maturing, when the first two types of reduction finally mellow the wine, producing esters, and precipitate tannins. Concurrent with the reduction, oxidation is also taking place.

Refermentation Sometimes an apparently stable wine will start fermenting again. This may be due to the slight aeration which the wine receives at racking (particularly if sulphite is not used), raising the temperature of the wine, or a malo-lactic reaction (not a true referment). There is no means of preventing a temporary sticking of a ferment, except by meticulous attention to technique.

Refrigeration for Clearing Many compounds are insoluble at low temperatures, e.g. potassium bitartrate in particular is totally insoluble at freezing point, and proteins also are precipitated by cooling. By cooling wine, hazes due to these faults can be cleared.

Rémuage The technique of gradually inverting champagne bottles at the end of the bottle ferment. At the same time as the inversion is increased, the bottle is twisted so that the yeast falls to the neck of the bottle whence it can be removed by dégorgement.

Reproduction The various biological systems of furthering and increasing the species. (See Binary Fission; Budding).

Residual Sugar The sugar remaining in a wine at the end of fermentation.

Rhubarb One of the few fruits to earn an entry to itself! This is because it contains oxalic acid, a by-product of its own metabolism. This is toxic in high concentrations but, practically, it rarely attains a high enough level to create problems. Normal acid control methods suffice. There is no need to first de-acidify and then add more acid. The main acid of the stem (the edible part) is malic, while in the poisonous leaves it is oxalic. Therefore do not use the leaves.

Rohament P A commercial preparation of pectin glycoside

Ropiness See Bacteria, Lactic Acid and Ropiness.

Rosé The colour of a wine which is pale pink to light red in tint. To obtain such a colour, pulp fermentation is best, stopping as soon as a sufficient depth of colour has been obtained.

Roses contain tannin and, in addition to the delicate shades they can confer on a wine, they are most useful for bouquet enhancement. Often they are used in conjunction with elderflowers.

Rot, Noble See Botrytis.

— S —

Saccharomyces The generic name for wine and beer yeasts.

Saccharometer Another name for the hydrometer.

Salts All metals form salts by combining with alkaline radicals. Some are insoluble (calcium salts or potassium bitartrate); some soluble (common salt); while some fall between these extremes and are partially soluble. The salts of importance to winemaking are the so-called nutrient salts. (See Additives; Nutrients).

Salt Spoon See Appendix XII.

Sauternes An unusual wine type, which is made from botrytised grapes. It has a high glycerine content and a higher alcohol content than most table wines. It has a residual sugar of up to 10%, and the final gravity may be as high as 40.

Seals Another name for bungs; corks; and closures.

Sec The French word meaning *dry*.

Secondary Fermentation The quiet phase of slow steady fermentation. It starts after the first vigorous ferment slows and it ends with the cessation of fermentation. There is no definite recognisable point at which the primary ends and the secondary ferment starts.

Sediment See Deposit; Lees.

Serving Spoon See Appendix XII.

Serving Wine revolves around choosing the right menu with the right wine. Following the choice of wine, it has either to be chilled (whites), or maybe decanted (certain reds), and allowed to 'breathe'. Removal of the capsule, drawing the cork, pouring a not overfull glass and tasting are the final steps, ensuring of course that the correct glasses are being used.

Settling Higher quality wines can be produced by pressing and sulphiting in the usual way. The must is then allowed to settle for 24–48 hours so that the fruit pulp can fall out of suspension. Following this, the clear juice is racked off the deposit. Commercial wines such as champagne are made in this way.

S.G. The abbreviation for specific gravity.

Sharpness The tasting term for an over acid wine.

Sherry A Spanish fortified wine. It varies from the pale dry fino to the dark brown sherries. Grapes, after plastering with gypsum, are pressed and fermented. During maturation, if lucky, a flor develops on the surface of the wine. Maturation is carried out in partially filled casks which are not closed, but merely protected from infection. The wine may be fortified to about 18% alcohol before maturing. It is the presence of a flor which, by preventing oxygen reaching the wine, ensures the pale colour of a Fino. If no flor develops, the sherry is oxidised to a dark colour.

Sherry Flor See Flor.

Sickness, Bottle See Bottle Sickness.

Sieve Nowadays best made of plastic, a sieve is invaluable in straining ingredients, with or without the aid of a straining cloth.

Sinker A heavy perforated plate which holds the cap of pulp below the surface during pulp fermentation. Its use helps prevent infection, and ensures complete extraction.

Siphoning See Racking.

Slime An exudate produced by both torulopsis and leuconostoc.

Soaking See Cold Extraction.

Social Wines There is no official definition as yet for this wine type. It is usually applied to a wine which is drinkable at any time without necessarily being accompanied by food. Thus this type of wine excudes aperitifs, brandy and port. Such wines should therefolre lie somewhere between a table and dessert wine in flavour, sweetness and alcoholic strength.

Soda, Washing A strong cleaning agent useful for removing stains and scale from filthy equipment. As with most cleaning agents, equipment needs thorough rinsing after using it.

Sodium A metal of vital importance to winemaking. Its main function is to provide cations (positively charged atoms) for salt formation.

Sodium Benzoate The commonly available form of benzoic acid.

Sodium Hydroxide The most widely used strong alkali. To the winemaker, its use is in the titration of a wine must, using a N/10 solution. (See Acidity Determination).

Sodium Hypochlorite The basis of bleach. When put into solution, it liberates poisonous chlorine. It is an excellent agent for removing stains and hard deposits. Take care not to inhale the irritant chlorine gas, and ensure thorough rinsing of equipment after its use. (See Quantan; Milton).

Sodium Metabisulphite The widely available form of the winemaker's 'sulphite'. In solution, it is broken down to bisulphite and then to sulphur dioxide gas.

Soft Fruit such as bananas, blackberry, gooseberry, the plum family and raspberry, are difficult to press, since this usually produces a mush rather than free juice. The best method of preparation is by pulp fermentation. Other soft fruit which may be pressed if desired are apricot, elderberries, grape and peach.

Solera The system of blending and maturing sherry. Casks are arranged in tiers, with the oldest wine at the lowest level. Wine ready for bottling is drawn from the bottom tier; some wine from each cask. This space is filled with wine drawn from the next tier up; after mixing the drawn wine, the casks are topped up. The process is continued to the top level, where the topping up is done with young wine from the bodega.

Solute A substance which is dissolved in a liquid

Sorbic Acid as the sodium or potassium salt is permitted in some branches of the food industry as an anti-bacterial agent. It is now a permitted fermentation inhibitor and should be used at a rate of 1 gram/gallon.

Sorbitol A hexose monosaccharide which is not fermented by wine yeasts and therefore can be used to sweeten a wine after fermentation has stopped. By using it, the chances of refermentation in an unstable wine are lessened.

Sour(ness) A tasting term used to describe the bitter acid taste of an acetified wine.

Sparkling Wine A wine which on being opened and poured effervesces due to the presence of dissolved carbon dioxide in the wine. This is achieved either by bottle or tank fermentation or by carbonation. The last is not recommended for amateurs to attempt.

Sparkling Wine, Alcohol Content should ideally be between 10–11% alcohol.

Sparkling Wine Charmat Process A method of secondary fermentation in a sealed tank after the base wine has been prepared in the usual manner. The quality of such wines is considered inferior to those produced in the traditional manner.

Sparkling Wines, Pressure in See Champagne Bottles, Pressure in.

Sparkling Wines, Transfer Process A method of production which allows for bottle fermentation, but obviates the need for the expensive rémuage and degorgement processes.

Specific Gravity The ratio of the density of a substance compared to water. The result is a figure without a unit. It is a bad term, since it is unrelated to gravity. A better term would be specific density. This measurement is the single most useful reading obtainable from a must or wine. From it can be calculated required sugar additions, alcohol content (potential or actual). (See Hydrometer).

Specific Gravity and Insolubles As far as the winemaker is concerned, the specific gravity gives a reading convertable to the sugar or alcohol content of the wine or must. However, a certain amount of this figure is due to insoluble substances present. All these will increase the specific gravity. To arrive at a more accurate reading, a fixed figure (which is purely arbitrary) should be subtracted from the reading obtained. This deductible amount is usually taken to be 0·007.

Specific Gravity and Sugar Content 1 lb of sugar dissolved in enough water to give a final volume of one gallon will have a specific gravity of 1·036. The full range of gravity and sugar contents is given in Appendix VI.

Specific Gravity and Temperature Every hydrometer has a temperature at which it reads accurately. This is etched upon it. If the temperature is higher than this, the reading will be too low because the liquid being measured expands. Similarly, if the temperature is lower, the reading is too high, due to contraction. (See Appendix VII for table of correcting factors).

Specific Gravity of Wines As a rough rule of thumb, a dry wine has a final gravity of 0·998 or less. Medium wines have a gravity between 0·998 and 1·010. Sweet table wines have a gravity up to 1·020 and sweet dessert wines may have a gravity as high as 1·040 (as do Sauternes, such as Chateau d'Yquem).

Spices are not so widely used today as in the past. Metheglin and other types of spiced mead, some aperitifs and liqueurs and hot spiced punches are the range of drinks to which spices are added. If using spice, do not add too much. It is better to add small amounts incrementally, until the desired taste is achieved, than to add too much at the outset.

Spirit Any distillate of alcohol containing a higher percentage of alcohol than the original mixture. *Distillation is illegal without a licence.*

Spirit, Additional When a sparkling wine has been dégorged, the loss is made up with a mixture of brandy (additional spirit) and syrup.

Spirit, Neutral Any distilled alcoholic beverage which does not have an overpowering flavour, e.g. vodka and Polish spirit. Both of these are ideal for fortification.

Spirit, Polish The most highly alcoholic drink commercially available. It has a proof of 120°, 130° or 140°. While it is correspondingly more expensive, the smaller volume required offsets the financial outlay. Since less is needed, less dilution of the base wine occurs.

Spirit, Proof In the United Kingdom, a mixture containing 100° proof alcohol is one which weighs 12/13 of an equal volume of water. 100° proof is equivalent to an alcohol content of 57·06%. The United States ratio is much simpler: 100° proof is equivalent to an alcohol content of 50%.

Spirit for Fortification See Fortification.

Spoilage See Actinic Action of Sunlight; Bacteria; Infection.

Spontaneous Fermentation The now démodé method of allowing the natural yeast on the ingredients or in the air to multiply and start a ferment. While this used to work reasonably well on the Continent, it had an unacceptably high rate of infection. In amateur circles, the failure rate was (and probably still is) even greater. For the few extra pence involved, it is better to buy a yeast culture and innoculate with this after sterilising the must, to prevent wild yeasts and spoilage organisms gaining a hold.

Spoon, Coffee; Egg; Dessert; Salt; Table; Tea See Appendix XII.

Spoon Sizes See Appendix XII.

Spores Some bacteria can, under adverse conditions, protect themselves from death by forming spores. These are tough walled structures which protect the nucleus. Once in a spore form, a bacterium can withstand extremes of temperature and environment for long periods of time. Yeasts can also form spores, and the way in which they do is part of the taxonomy of the species.

Stabilising The stopping of fermentation and prevention of refermentation in the presence of residual sugar. (See Racking; Sodium Benzoate; Sorbic Acid).

Stabilising by Racking By the time fermentation is completed there is a sizeable deposit at the bottom of the container. This contains, in addition to debris and insoluble salts, a large viable population of yeast cells. If a sweet wine is desired, racking the wine from this deposit before the end of fermentation will obviously remove a large number of live yeast cells which might otherwise continue fermenting. If this racking is followed by sulphiting and another racking after a week or ten days, virtually all the live yeast cells will be removed from the wine, so that a stable sweet wine will result.

Stabilising with Sulphite After racking a wine that is not completely clear, there are inevitably some live yeast cells remaining. In order to inhibit these from further reproduction and alcohol production, they must be inhibited by the addition of sulphite. The recommended amount is 100 ppm at the first racking, and 50 ppm at successive rackings.

Stable A wine is said to be stable when there is no further chance of continuing fermentation.

Starch is composed of long branching chains of glucose molecules joined together. If present in a wine it will cause a haze and, in order to prevent this, it is important to use a starch-destroying enzyme (Amylase) when the recipe includes any starch-containing fruit or vegetables, such as cereals and potatoes. Wine yeasts do not contain an enzyme capable of breaking down starch.

Starch Enzymes See Amylase.

Starch Haze See Grain; Haze, Starch.

Starch, Test for See Iodine.

Starter Most yeast cultures contain sufficient yeast to start a must of between 1–2 gallons. If a larger amount of wine is being prepared, it is essential to prepare a starter in order to give the must the greatest possible chance of a successful fermentation. To prepare a starter, take ½ pint of boiling water and add 15 g of dried malt, 15 g sugar, 2 g diammonium phosphate and citric acid. When this is cooled to between 75–80°F, the yeast may be added. The sterile container in which this is placed must be plugged with sterile cotton wool, and when this starter is fully active it may be added to the bulk of the must.

Steam Extraction Fruit placed in a flow of steam will be broken down so that the juice may be easily extracted. However, the use of steam must be limited in time, otherwise the ingredients may suffer from overcooking.

Steeping See Cold Extraction.

Sterilant Any chemical which either inhibits or kills micro-organisms.

Sterilizing The addition of a sterilant to kill or inhibit unwanted organisms either in the equipment or in the must, or the use of heat for the same purpose.

Sterilizing Bottles Following thorough cleansing and rinsing of bottles, sterilizing is achieved by swilling them out with a weak solution of sulphite.

Sterilizing, Chemical The chief sterilizing agent to the winemaker is metabisulphite, whose active agent is sulphur dioxide gas. For most equipment and ingredients, a 2% solution is adequate.

Sterilizing Corks Do not boil corks, since this makes them hard and liable to break. It is best to soak them for an hour in a 1% solution of sulphite. The addition of a few drops of glycerine will help lubricate them so that insertion is easier.

Sterilizing Detergents A new range of chemicals on the market which are very useful for equipment, since they perform simultaneous cleansing and sterilizing. Despite the claim that many of these are both odourless and tasteless, it is important to ensure a thorough rinsing after their use, in case this should not be true.

Sterilizing Equipment Rinsing equipment thoroughly in 1% or 2% sulphite solution is quite adequate, providing that the solution still smells strongly of sulphur dioxide. The solution should not be kept for more than a few months.

Sterilizing by Heat Although this is theoretically one of the most effective means of sterilizing, it is also one of the most dangerous. Plastics not intended for high temperatures will melt, and glass suddenly exposed to high temperatures will suddenly break due to thermal shock. Unprotected hands will be burnt severely. With this method it is best to stick to small items which can be boiled, either in a small saucepan or in a pressure cooker.

Sterilizing Musts In order to prevent volatilisation of ingredients and over-extraction of pectin, it is best to avoid boiling wherever possible. (Vegetables are the exception to this.) The safest, most effective method of sterilizing is the use of sulphite at a concentration of 50 ppm. This is added to the must 24 hours prior to pitching the yeast, by when the majority of sulphur dioxide will have evaporated. Another advantage of sulphur dioxide is that it does not kill, but merely inhibits yeast.

Sterilizing by Radiation This is of no importance in the home, but it is used in small doses by some companies in the preparation of yeast cultures to ensure a pure strain.

Sterilizing with Sulphite is undoubtedly the best if one has to choose a single method of sterilizing. It is cheap, easy to carry out and it is, above all, effective. To all intents and purposes, sulphite does not react with any of the winemaking equipment to cause damage, with the exception of rubber corks which, if left exposed for a long time, eventually become white and brittle. For most purposes, a 1% or 2% solution is adequate, except for storing sterile containers which should contain a few mls of 10% solution and be kept tightly corked. This will mean emptying the container prior to use. Rinsing with sterile tap water will ensure continuing sterile conditions.

Sticking Any fermentation which ceases at a gravity of above 30 may be considered to be stuck. Below this, the wine may be usable as a sweet wine.

Sticking and Acid Imbalance The presence of adequate citric acid is of importance in ensuring a healthy primary ferment. Approximately 1½ ppt of the total acid should be added as citric. It is also important not to have too acid a must, otherwise the ferment may be slowed.

Sticking and Alcohol Content All yeasts have a point after which the production of further alcohol will cause death of the yeast. Most wine yeasts are capable of producing about 16% alcohol although, with careful exponential feeding, it is possible to achieve a higher figure. If a high alcohol content wine is wanted, do not add all the sugar at the outset, but rather in small amounts so that, should sticking occur, an over-sweet wine will not result.

Sticking and Antiseptics See Citrus Peel and Inhibition; Sticking and Sulphite.

Sticking and Infection Should a yeast become contaminated, bacterial off-flavours will develop as well as a sufficiently large bacterial colony to inhibit the establishment of a fermentative yeast colony. Usually, the formation of such off-flavours precludes the production of a drinkable wine.

Sticking and Metal Deficiency is a rare phenomenon, since most ingredients contain sufficient trace elements for fermentation. Occasionally, if the water supply is lacking in magnesium, sticking may occur, and the addition of magnesium sulphate (Epsom Salts), ½ g per gallon, will overcome this problem.

Sticking and Must Imbalance The manufacture of leaf and flower wines are notorious in this respect, since the ingredients contain almost no ammonium salts or vitamin B. When using such ingredients, it is important to ensure adequate use of additives.

Sticking and Nutrient Deficiency In order to allow the yeast to build up sufficient protein for itself as well as to ensure the presence of potassium and phosphate salts, the use of nutrients is important.

Sticking and Old Yeast Although a yeast culture contains yeast which is in the resting phase, there will, even when under ideal storage conditions, be a decrease in viable cells so that eventually a healthy ferment cannot be started.

Sticking and Small Yeast Colony See Starters.

Sticking and Sugar Excess The addition of too much sugar initially to a must will cause rupturing of the yeast cells and, in order to prevent this, exponential feeding is recommended. (See Osmosis).

Sticking and Sulphite If excess sulphite is used to sterilize the must and the yeast pitched too soon, the yeast may be killed rather than merely inhibited by the sulphur dioxide. To prevent this, no more than 100 ppm sulphur dioxide should be used for sterilizing, and a period of 24–48 hours should have elapsed before adding the yeast.

Sticking and Temperature At a temperature below 55°F yeast cells tend to become dormant. Above 85°F the yeast cells and their enzymes are denatured and killed. It is important to remember that fermentation itself gives out heat, so that although the air surrounding the fermentation may appear cool enough it is quite possible that within the fermentation jar the temperature is dangerously high. Much better to ensure a temperature a few degrees below the ideal to allow for this.

Sticking and Undissolved Substances Sugar in particular, if added undissolved to a must, may inhibit the yeast by the building up of a layer of syrup at the bottom of the jar. This will then destroy the greater part of the yeast colony. To avoid this, it is important to add substances in liquid form.

Sticking and Vitamin Deficiency Many vitamins are essential to yeast reproduction and, apart from vitamin B_1, most are present in ingredients. Thus it is important to use vitamin B_1, about 3 mgs per gallon, in order to prevent sticking. In particular, flowers and leaves are lacking in this vitamin.

Still, Distillation Appartus ranging from frankly dangerous and illegal to highly specialised 'towers', which can separate any number of chemicals out of a mixture. This principle has wide ranging applications, though it is specially useful in the making of whisky!

Still Wine can be defined as a wine which does not contain carbon dioxide in solution, and therefore does not effervesce when opened. In other words, (to be Johnsonian!) the opposite of sparkling.

Stock Solutions Solutions containing a known weight per unit volume of a chemical compound. They are of particular use in measuring small weights of additives.

Stock Solution, Acid Some authorities advocate the use of a mixture of acids in solution form but, whether a mixture or single acid is put into solution, the use of 1 oz of acid in $1\frac{1}{2}$ pints will give a solution of which 1 fluid oz contains 1 g of acid.

Stock Solution, Sugar To avoid the possibility of sticking, it is best to use sugar in syrup form. To make this, 2 lb of sugar to 1 pint of water is used. The mixture should be boiled for a short time until clear and should not be used until cool. One pint of this syrup will then add one pound of sugar to the must. The shelf life of such a solution is fairly short. Therefore it is best to prepare small amounts of syrup at a time.

Stock Solution, Sulphite A solution containing 5% by weight of sulphur dioxide is prepared by dissolving 4 oz of metabisulphite to a total volume of 2 pints. 5 ml of such a solution added to a gallon gives a dose of 50 ppm.

Stone Fruit e.g. Apricot, bullace, cherry, damson, peach, plum and sloe. These fruits are best prepared by stoning, lightly crushing and pulp fermenting, thus ensuring adequate tannin and flavour extraction.

Stoneware See Containers, Earthenware.

Stopper Any device used to close a container. (See Bung; Closure; Cork).

Storage When fermenting, wines need to be kept at a constant temperature of between 60–70°F, and during maturation are ideally kept at a temperature of 55°F. Bottle racks, as well as maturing containers, need to be kept at 55°F in an atmosphere which is free from light and which is dry. Dampness will predispose to mould infections.

Storage Containers For most amateur winemakers it is hard to beat the glass, clear or opaque, one gallon jars, which, other than for bulk producers, will suffice for virtually all wines. (See Containers; Casks).

Straining A means of separating pulp from juice. On most occasions racking will suffice, but a large loose deposit in a freshly pulped fruit may prove difficult to separate and therefore the use of a sieve or straining cloth will be found to be invaluable.

Straining Cloth See Cloth, Straining.

Strong Acid See Acid, Strong.

Suberin The natural 'glue' which holds cork together. As it is slightly soluble in alcohol in concentrations above that of table wines, it has become the practice to store fortified wines upright. Port, on the other hand, is stored on its side, but the problem of cork dissolution is minimised by the additional seal of wax over the cork.

Substrate The base liquid in which a substance is dissolved. For example, in a syrup solution the water is the substrate and the sugar the solute.

Succinic Acid A by-product of fermentation whose major function in winemaking is in the ester formation which occurs during maturation. As this acid is now available commercially it is a good practice to add a small amount per gallon after the final racking, prior to maturation. It is important to realise, however, that a reasonable length of time must be allowed for the chemical changes to occur and that the mere addition of this acid does not automatically confer an improved bouquet on a wine. See Appendix X for the chemical reactions whereby this acid is present in wines.

Sucrase The enzyme which breaks down sucrose to its component sugars, glucose and fructose. Since this enzyme is secreted by wine yeasts, there is no need either to use invert sugar or to invert the sugar prior to its use.

Sucrose The most commonly used sugar in winemaking. It is a hexose-disaccharide, composed of one molecule of glucose and one of fructose. After being inverted, or broken into its constituent monosaccharides, it then enters the fermentation pathway and both hexoses are eventually metabolised to alcohol and carbon dioxide. The sources of this sugar are cane sugar and beet sugar. It does not matter in what form sucrose, or sugar, as it is usually referred to, is added to a wine, as long as the packet says that it is pure. Against this, the champagne producers claim that when they top up a champagne after dégorgement the use of beet sugar confers an earthy taste on the wine. There is, however, no definite proof either way to this statement. Other forms of sucrose are the various brown sugars, lump sugar, etc. etc., but as far as the winemaker is concerned the use of ordinary granulated sugar is sufficient.

Sugar Apart from the fruit, vegetable, leaf or flower base ingredient, sugar is the most expensive ingredient to be used in winemaking. Indeed, if home-grown produce is used, this and grape concentrate are the chief cost factors. Its use is essential since no fruit, other than the grape, consistently have a high enough sugar content to produce a wine with a sufficient alcohol content. Sugar should be added to the must after assay of the natural sugar content and, ideally, should be added in stages. (See Exponential Feeding.)

Sugar Additions   See Exponential Feeding.

Sugar Amounts   The quantity of sugar required in a must should be worked out on the basis that 1 lb of sugar in a gallon will raise the gravity by 36. From this figure and the specific gravity of the juice (extrapolated to a reading for one gallon), the amount of sugar required to raise the gravity to the desired starting gravity can be calculated.

Sugar Beet   The vegetable discovered by Napoleon's scientists to contain a high percentage of sucrose. It is today the source of approximately 30% of household sugar consumed in this country. It is also a vegetable which can be used as a base ingredient for a wine.

Sugar, Brown   Sugars which are heated lose their normal molecular structure and in so doing change from a white translucent colour to a brown colour. This amorphous structure (caramel) is the cause for the change in colour. The use of caramel in a wine intended for the table is not to be recommended, since the flavour is not sufficiently subtle. However, for wines intended in particular as dessert wines, it has a definite value.

Sugar, Cane   See Cane Sugar.

Sugar, Caramel   See Caramel.

Sugar Classification   See Classification of Sugar.

Sugar Content of Dry Wines   The basic definition of a dry wine was one which contained no sugar to the taste. However, with the use of Clinitest tablets now commonly applied to wine assessment, it has been proposed that the definition of a dry wine should be one in which there is less than 1% residual sugar.

Sugar Estimation in Wine The old test reagents of Fehlings solution have been superseded by Clinitest tablets. To perform the estimation, 5 drops of wine and 10 drops of water are placed in a dry test tube and one test tablet dropped into the test tube. After the fizzing has stopped, the colours are compared with the supplied chart. If the reading is over the 2% mark the wine must be diluted and the test repeated.

Sugar, Feeding Yeast with   See Exponential Feeding.

Sugar, Fermentable   See Fermentable Base.

Sugar and Fermentation   The presence of sugar in a solution containing live yeast cells in anaerobic conditions is the basis of fermentation to produce alcohol. The basic formula is that one molecule of a hexomonosaccharide is broken down to two molecules of carbon dioxide and two of ethyl alcohol. For the full series of reactions, see Appendix IX.

Sugar Haze   A misnomer, for in fact the haze is usually due to yeast. This haze is usually in a stuck ferment in which the sugar content is too high. (See Osmosis; Haze, Yeast).

Sugar, Honey   One pound of honey contains as near as matters 1 lb of sugar and can therefore, if desired, be substituted for sugar in a recipe. Care must be taken, however, not to use a strongly scented honey, such as from eucalyptus, which may confer unpleasant tastes on the wine.

Sugar, Inversion of   Contrary to the belief of many people, the wine yeast secretes the enzyme invertase, which breaks down sucrose to its component glucose and fructose molecules. If, however, it is desired to use invert sugar, this can be made by the production of a sugar solution and the addition of $\frac{1}{8}$ oz of tartaric acid. This solution should be boiled for about 10 minutes. Despite some people's claims that the use of invert sugar produces a better wine, there is very little scientific evidence to support this, and indeed most authorities are convinced that cane sugar, logically, since yeast contains invertase, is quite adequate for the production of quality wines.

Sugar, Invert A sugar solution in which the sucrose has been broken down to its component sucrose and fructose molecules. If using invert sugar, it is important to remember that '50% more sugar' should be used, since in the breaking down of sucrose to glucose and fructose, water is taken up, so that one pound of invert sugar is only two-thirds as sweet as cane sugar.

Sugar, Lactose See Lactose.

Sugar Measuring The standard method of measuring or assessing the quantity of sugar in a must is by the use of the hydrometer. The specific gravity of the juice extrapolated to the final volume gives the measure of sugar in pounds per gallon, if the answer is divided by 36. Most authorities agree that it is necessary to subtract 7 from the gravity to allow for suspended particles and insolubles in the must.

Sugar, Natural See Natural Sugar.

Sugar, Residual The remaining sugar in a finished wine. For a dry wine, this should be less than 1% as measured by dextro-check. Medium and sweet wines usually have their residual sugar expressed as a gravity, since the percentage of sugar varies considerably. A medium wine usually has a gravity of 0·998–1·010, and a sweet wine a gravity above that.

Sugar and Specific Gravity One pound of sugar in a solution of 1 gallon in volume will have a specific gravity of 36. To all intents and purposes, apart from the arbitrary figure of 7 (the specific gravity allowed for suspended solids), the specific gravity of a must or wine is entirely due to the sugar content.

Sugar Syrup is prepared by heating 1 pint of water with 2 lb of sugar. This is then allowed to boil for a few minutes, until clear, and, when cool, it may be used. The use of 1 pt of this syrup will add 1 lb of sugar to the must.

Sugar, Testing for See Sugar Estimation in Wine.

Sugar Types See Classification of Sugar.

Sugar Volume Two pounds of sugar occupy a volume of 1 pt. Thus a syrup composed of 2 lb of sugar and 1 pt of water will result in a syrup of which 1 pt contains 1 lb of sugar.

Sulfite The American spelling of Sulphite. (See Sulphite).

Sulfur The American spelling of sulphur. (See Sulphur).

Sulphate is usually present in adequate amounts from the water supply, but if lacking can be added as magnesium sulphate (Epsom Salts), 0·5 g per gallon. Other than this trace amount required for normal fermentation, sulphate is required in large amounts as calcium sulphate (gypsum) in the production of sherry.

Sulphite The term used loosely to cover sodium or potassium metabisulphite, and bisulphites, sulphites, or sulphur dioxide gas. All these substances are derived from the first two and are merely breakdown products of these compounds. For ease of expression, sulphiting has come to be the addition of sulphur dioxide either as Campden tablets or as metabisulphite salts to a wine or a must. One of the chief reasons that sulphite is such a successful sterilizing agent for the winemaker is that it is effective against all known infections in wine and in concentrations as used it has little or no effect against yeast. Its use at a concentration of 100 ppm when preparing the must is effective in either killing or inhibiting all unwanted bacteria until the alcohol production commences when that takes over as the chief bacterial agent. In the concentrations used it is non-toxic to man.

Sulphite and Acid Sulphite, when put into aqueous solution, forms sulphurous acid, and this raises the acidity (by only a small amount) which, for practical purposes, can be ignored.

Sulphite and Ageing The action of sulphite in a maturing wine is that of an anti-oxidant and therefore should only be used for white wines. The action of sulphite is the taking up of oxygen by combining with sulphur dioxide to form sulphur trioxide, which is then converted to sulphuric acid. To prevent too great a quantity of acid being formed, no more than 50 ppm should be added prior to maturation. Red wines should not need sulphiting, as they have sufficient anti-oxidant properties in themselves, unless of course infected. (See Volatile Acids).

Sulphite and Anti-Oxidation In solution, sulphite liberates sulphur dioxide gas. This combines with oxygen to form sulphur trioxide, which then combines with further oxygen to form sulphurous acid. This then combines with water to form sulphuric acid. The routine use of sulphite when racking any wine except sherry is to be commended, since it will prevent o-polyphenoloxidase darkening, and will also prevent over oxidation of the wine. The normal amounts to use are 100 ppm at the first racking, and 50 ppm at successive rackings.

Sulphite and Clarification The addition of sulphite at racking aids clarification firstly by inhibition of the re-establishment of the yeast colony and secondly by neutralising some of the electrical charges on colloidal suspensions.

Sulphite and Extraction Sulphite has no action as such as an extraction agent, but its use is imperative in cold water methods of extraction to prevent infection.

Sulphite and Glycerol Formation Over-sulphiting a must prior to innoculation will result in its combining with acetaldehyde, thus blocking the formation of some of the alcohol. This is another reason for not over-sulphiting for sterilization purposes. The addition of sulphite after fermentation has commenced does not result in this additional glycerol formation, since the pathways have already been set up and metabolism can continue as normally.

Sulphite and Oxidation See Sulphite and Anti-oxidation.

Sulphite and Racking See Sulphite and Anti-Oxidation; Sulphite and Clarification.

Sulphite Solution, Stability of As long as it is kept in a tightly stoppered bottle and the solution still smells of sulphite, it will be effective. However, to be safe, it is best not to keep it for longer than 3–4 months, as it will inevitably become diluted as damp equipment is rinsed with it.

Sulphite and Sterilization See Sterilizing and Sulphite.

Sulphite Stock Solution Four ounces of metabisulphite made into a solution with a volume of two pints will produce a 5% solution with respect to sulphur dioxide.

Sulphite, Tolerance of Yeast to While not being killed by high sulphite concentrations, yeast is inhibited by sulphite in concentrations above 100 ppm and it is for this reason that 24–48 hours should elapse before pitching the yeast.

Sulphur Small amounts of sulphur are required as a metal by yeasts in building up certain of their proteins, and sufficient of this can be obtained from the sterilizing dose of sulphite. Until the introduction of metabisulphite salts, the use of sulphur wicks was widespread as the sterilizing agent.

Sulphur Candles The old sterilizing method for equipment was to burn wicks or candles of sulphur inside the equipment. The use of this is dangerous to the wine, since sulphur tends to drip. Where it comes into contact with wood it impregnates the wood with resultant hydrogen sulphide formation, which imparts a 'rotten eggs' taste to the wine.

Sulphur Dioxide This gas is obtained by the breakdown of metabisulphite salts to bisulphite and then to sulphite. The latter compound releases sulphur dioxide gas, which effectively kills or inhibits all unwanted bacterial infections. It is possible to obtain sulphur dioxide in liquid or gaseous form, but for the amateur winemaker it is best used as sulphite.

Sulphur, Test for This is possible using a special cylinder, together with a special solution to titrate the wine for sulphur dioxide content. The main purpose of this test is to ensure an adequate sulphur dioxide level in a wine so that it is less likely to undergo over-oxidation or oxidative discolouration.

Sulphur Trioxide An unstable sulphur compound formed when sulphur dioxide combines with any free oxygen in the must. The sulphur trioxide then combines with water to form sulphurous and then sulphuric acid.

Sulphuric Acid One of the three strong acids. Its main importance in winemaking is as a unit for acidity measurement.

Sulphurous Acid An unstable acid containing sulphur which is able to combine with acetaldehyde to form a compound blocking the production of alcohol, if sulphite is added prior to fermentation. If formed by sulphiting at racking time, the formation of this acetaldehyde-sulphite compound is valuable in preventing oxidative changes.

Sultanas (U.S.A. White Raisins). See Raisins.

Sunlight See Actinic Action of Sunlight.

Sweet Wine A wine is said to be sweet if it tastes obviously sweet to the palate, and if its final gravity is above 1·020. Indeed, commercial wines such as Chateau d'Yquem have a final gravity of 1·040.

Sweeteners, Artificial See Lactose; Potassium Sorbate; Saccharin.

Sweetness A subjective taste experience dependant on the quantity of residual sugar in a wine, and the sensitivity of the taster's palate.

Sweetening with Non-Fermentable Sugars is possible by using sugars which are not fermented by wine yeasts, e.g. arabinose or lactose. From the point of view of availability, the latter is the better choice.

Synthetics See Containers, Plastic.

Syphoning The technique of taking off a liquid from a sediment by means of a tube wherein the atmospheric pressure upon the liquid to be syphoned acts as the motive power to propel the liquid through the tube. This will occur once the tube has been filled by suction and maintained by the tube being kept below the level of the liquid in the upper container.

Syrup Either a drink or a solution containing a high sugar content. For the winemaker, syrup is usually taken to mean a solution of sugar containing 1 lb per pint.

— T —

Table Spoon See Appendix XII.

Table Wine A table wine is red, rosé or white in colour, containing between 9–12% alcohol; of a light to medium body, and usually medium to dry in taste. It is important that the flavour and bouquet of a table wine does not overpower the food it is chosen to accompany.

Tablet, Campden One of the commonly available forms of sulphite. One Campden tablet per gallon will give a concentration of 50 ppm sulphur dioxide gas.

Taint Any off-flavour or taste produced by infection or poor fermentative technique.

Tank Fermenting A commercial method of sparkling wine production wherein the costly process of rémuage and dégorgement are obviated by the secondary fermentation taking place in a sealed tank, rather than in the bottle. See Cuvée Close.

Tank Process See Tank Fermenting.

Tannic Acid A generic name for the various forms of tannin.

Tannin The group of phenol-based plant acids which are essential to give 'zest' to a wine.

Tannin and Antisepsis Although not sufficient to sterilize a must, tannins do have a slight antiseptic property.

Tannin and Clarification Tannin is able to join with protein to form insoluble coagulates, thus clearing a protein haze. In addition to this, tannin, bearing an electrical charge, is able to neutralise an oppositely charged colloidal haze and so promote clarification. It is because of these two actions of tannin that red wines tend to clear more rapidly than white wines, since the former contain more tannin.

Tannin, Classification There are two main types of tannins:
(1) **Hydrolizable,** which have ester-like properties and can be broken down by hydrolysis reactions.

(2) **Condensed,** where the components of the compound are bound together by carbon linkages.

Tannin, Content of Fruit Apples, elderberries and plums are the highest tannin carrying fruits the winemaker uses.

Tannin, Content of Red Wine is between 0·1–0·3 g%. This probably also includes a certain amount of colouring matter as well as the astringent tasting tannins. (See Tannin Occurrence).

Tannin Extraction is achieved by pulp fermentation. In order to maximise it the cap of pulp must be regularly broken up and stirred into the must.

Tannin and Fining If an albumin type of fining agent such as egg-white or gelatin is chosen, it is important to ensure adequate tannin content in the wine, since these agents combine with tannin to precipitate protein-tannin complexes. Elderberry wines in particular, which tend to be harsh when young, can be mellowed by this means; hence making them drinkable far younger.

Tannin, Grape The commercially available compound of tannin.

Tannin and Inhibition Tannin is an enzyme inhibitor to some of the metabolic systems, particularly in the prevention of oxidative casse.

Tannin and Maturing During maturation the tannin content of a wine falls as it combines with aldehydes or precipitates in combination with protein. The length of time for the tannin to fall to a palatable level also ensures that the other components of the wine mellow. Thus, a better matured wine is often obtained by the addition of some tannin prior to final maturation if the wine is low in tannin.

Tannin Measurement is a difficult procedure for the amateur winemaker.

Tannin Occurrence Tannin occurs chiefly in the skin, stems and seeds of plants. In the grape, the seed contains 5–6% of the total tannin; the stem 3%; and the skin between 0·5 and 1·5%. The free run juice of white grapes usually contains less than 0·02% of tannin.

Tannin and Taste The greater part of the astringency due to tannin is from gallic and ellagic acids. If desired, they can be reduced by fining.

Tannin and Tea The British panacea for all ills contains large amounts of tannin but, like most readily available sources of additives, it is not a very precise means of balancing a wine. It is far better to use commercially prepared tannin so that a precise amount may be added.

Tannin, Types of   d - catectol
                  l - epicatechol
                  l - epigallocatechol
                  dl - gallocatechol
                  d - epicatecholgallate.

Tannin and Yeast Growth It is possible that the presence of excessive tannin may inhibit yeast growth. This is thought to be more true of wild yeasts than wine yeasts.

Tartar, Cream of See Cream of Tartar.

Tartaric Acid is the principal grape acid in the ripe fruit. Because of this authorities are in agreement that its use is invaluable in quality wine production. It is particularly valuable during maturation, where it freely enters ester forming reactions. If present in excess, it will tend to form potassium bitartrate or even argols.

Tartaric Acid Reduction Since tartaric acid combines easily with potassium, the addition of potassium carbonate will result in the precipitation of Cream of Tartar, if it is desired to lower the tartaric acid level. This is particularly valuable when using British grapes, which tend to be high in acid. One gram of potassium carbonate will lower the tartaric acid content by about two parts per thousand. Similarly, calcium carbonate can be used to lower the acidity, if desired.

Taste is composed of four elements: sweetness, saltiness, acidity and bitterness. The other components of a wine are detected by the nose. (See Bouquet; Palate).

Tasting The series of steps taken in the appreciation of a wine are, firstly, to examine its clarity and colour; then to sniff the bouquet; and finally to taste it with the palate. A good wine is one which is perfectly clear, of a pleasing colour and pleasant bouquet, and which tastes equally pleasant; wherein no one flavour predominates. In other words, to be a good wine, it should be balanced.

Tawny One of the classes of port. This particular class of port is cask matured for considerable periods of time so that the colour oxidises from its initial purple colour to a tawny brown colour. The wine is said to have a woody flavour and a bouquet which is often described as nutty.

Taxation See Duty.

Tea Spoon See Appendix XII.

Tea and Tannin See Tannin in Tea.

Temperature It is most important to control closely the temperature of all stages of winemaking.

Temperature and Clearing A haze due to cream of tartar will be rapidly cleared by chilling the wine, since this is insoluble at low temperatures. Similarly, proteins coagulate near freezing point.

Temperature Control It is important at all stages of winemaking to have a close control on temperature. If no specially constructed thermostatically controlled unit is available, then choose a part of the house where a constant temperature is maintained for most of the year, e.g. a heated cupboard.

Temperature and Fermentation Most wine yeasts are completely inhibited below a temperature of 45°F and killed by temperatures above 90°F. The optimum temperature for fermentation is about 80°F during the lag phase; 70°F during primary fermentation and 60°F for the secondary ferment.

Temperature and Madeira Madeira is a white wine which obtains its characteristic caramelised flavour from being 'cooked' in an Estufagem at high temperatures for varying periods of time. The higher the temperature (often as high as 140°F), the shorter the time of 'cooking' and the lower the quality of the wine. For a high quality wine, a temperature of 90°F is used for periods of up to a year.

Temperature and Maturing The optimum temperature for maturing wines is about 55°F.

Temperature and Specific Gravity Hydrometers are only accurate at one temperature, which is indicated on that instrument. If the temperature of the test liquid is above or below this, corrections have to be made to the reading. See Appendix VII for the table of corrections.

Temperature for Storage 55°F is considered best for this purpose. See Maturation Temperature.

Test for Alcohol Content An approximate result can be obtained by dividing the *total* gravity drop by a factor dependant on the starting gravity (see Appendix IV(a)). However, a very much more accurate method, which is simple, is as follows: 200 mls of wine are boiled down to about half the volume to drive off the alcohol. The volume of the cooled wine is then restored by adding distilled water. The specific gravity of the wine must be taken before boiling and again after making it to volume. The increase in gravity is noted and a factor of 0·16 is added in all cases. This figure is known as the spirit indication, and is subtracted from 1,000 to give the specific gravity of the dilute alcohol in the wine. From the spirit indication tables in Appendix I V(b), the alcohol content of the wine can be ascertained.

Test for Bottling Readiness This test is intended for white wines which may develop a protein haze after bottling. Add

1·5 mls of 5% tannic acid to 25 mls of wine. If a flocculate develops, the wine is liable to form a protein haze after bottling. The wine then needs trial fining prior to bulk treatment.

Test for Sulphur Dioxide See Sulphur Test for

Test for Hazes See Test for infection; Diagnosis of Faults, Appendix XI.

Test for Infection Samples of suspect wine are placed in two sterile jars. The first is sealed immediately, while the second is placed in a small amount of boiling water with the top loose for a few minutes. After removing, the top is screwed down. If a haze develops or becomes greater, in the first, while the second remains unchanged, then infection is proved.

Test for Iron A wine exhibiting a white or blue haze, together with a metallic taste can be suspected of being contaminated with iron. The addition of a pinch of metabisulphite will cause a yellowish deposit if this is so. If this confirmatory test is positive, it is not recommended that the amateur attempts curative action beyond a trial fining with 5% citric acid solution. If this does not aid clearing of the wine, it is best if the wine is discarded. The only effective method of iron removal is by the highly toxic potassium ferrocyanide. (See Hydrogen Peroxide).

Test for Natural Sugar is carried out by taking the specific gravity of the expressed juice from the ingredients. The reading obtained is then extrapolated to the final volume of the wine.

Test for Pectin To 5 ml of wine add 15 ml of methylated spirit. The presence of pectin will be confirmed by the formation of small clots in the test sample.

Test for pH The simplest method for the amateur is to use narrow range pH papers. A small drop of wine is placed on the strip of paper and, after the colour has developed, it is compared with a result chart.

Test for Protein Stability See Test for Bottling Readiness.

Test for Residual Sugar Using Clinitest tablets, place 5 drops of wine in a clean dry test tube. Add 10 drops of water. Add one tablet and after the fizzing has stopped, compare the colour developed with the colour chart provided. If the result is above 2%, dilute the wine and repeat the test. (See Clinitest; and Appendix VIII).

Test for Specific Gravity See Hydrometer.

Test for Starch See Iodine.

Test for Total Acidity See Acidity Determination.

Thermal Shock A phenomenon seen when an object is either rapidly heated or cooled. If sufficiently great, it may cause breakage of the object. This is seen particularly with glass equipment.

Thermometer An essential piece of equipment for the control of temperature and the correction of specific gravity readings For winemaking, it is best to have one that has a range from between 0–220°F, so that it may also be used for the preparation of syrups.

Thermostat A useful piece of equipment to use in conjunction with a heater. It works by switching on and off the heater when the temperature falls below or rises above the preset temperature.

Thiamine Hydrochloride Another name for Vitamin B.

Thin(ness) A tasting term meaning lacking in body. This is usually due to insufficient base fruit in the recipe. Using grape concentrate will help minimise this fault.

Ties, Wire See Muselet.

Titratable Acidity See Acidity, Titratable.

Titration The technique of measuring the acid content of a solution by the addition of an alkali, using an indicator to show the 'end point'. (See Acidity Determination).

Tolerance The term applied to the ability of a yeast to withstand a certain alcohol concentration before being inhibited by the alcohol. One of the hallmarks of a good yeast is the ability to withstand a high alcohol content.

Topping Up The practice of making up the loss of wine at racking. This can either be done with tap water (not a good practice, since it dilutes the alcohol and taste). A syrup of the same specific gravity as the wine can be used, but the same drawbacks apply. Best of all is to use a topping up wine of the same alcohol content as the wine. Obviously, it must be neutral in taste.

Topping Up Wine Any neutral tasting wine suitable for topping up purposes. If making such a wine, it is best to use simply a sugar solution of the desired starting gravity, together with the necessary additives and yeast. This wine should be cared for in the same manner as any other wine.

Torulopsis One of the species of slime forming yeasts. (See Diagnosis, Appendix XI).

Total Fermentable Base The term used to cover *all* the sugar in a must. This includes natural and added sugars. In addition, some of the degraded pectin is included in this class.

Tourne A lacto-bacillus infection occurring in tartaric acid containing wines. It causes a bitter off-flavour. Prevention is by attention to hygiene and anaerobic conditions. If this should occur, there is not much chance of salvaging the wine. (See Diagnosis, Appendix XI).

Toxic Materials Now that cadmium-containing plastics have been found to be less toxic than was at one time suggested, the only materials to constitute a real danger are lead and copper-containing materials.

Transfer Process See Sparkling Wine, Transfer Process.

Trial Fining Before fining a wine in bulk, it is always best to make a series of solutions of varying strengths of the fining agent and to add them in measured amounts to known small volumes of the wine. The solution which gives the best result or the minimum concentration of fining agent is chosen for bulk use.

Trial Tube A glass tube open at both ends, which is large enough to contain a hydrometer. Wine is sucked into the tube until the hydrometer floats, and the upper end of the tube is then occluded by a finger. The tube is lifted partially out of the test liquid until the column of liquid is at a convenient height for reading. Do not lift the base of the tube out of the liquid or the sample will fall back into the jar. The advantage of this piece of equipment is that it obviates the need to pour test liquids into hydrometer jars before testing.

Tribasic The adjective applied to acids which have three hydrogen ions available for dissociation in solution.

Triose A three-carbon sugar. They are formed during the breakdown of sugars, when one molecule of monosaccharide is broken into two molecules of triose. (See Fermentation Pathways, Appendix IX).

Tubing Essential equipment for racking wines. It is best in this day and age of plastics, to use an inert polythene which, in addition to being non-reactive, will not absorb flavours and will not discolour easily. The length needed depends on personal requirements. Tubing of $\frac{1}{4}$ in internal diameter is quite adequate for the purpose.

Tube Culture One of the available forms of yeast which is in liquid suspension. It requires activation by means of a starter.

Twaddell A unit of gravity wherein one unit equals 5 units on the specific gravity scale.

Types of Wine See Classification of Wine.

— U —

Ullage The air space between the level of the wine in a container and the cork. In the bottle, it should be between $\frac{1}{4}$ in and $\frac{1}{2}$ in, while in casks or jars it should be kept to the minimum consistent with an allowance for expansion.

Ultra Filter A filter capable of removing very small particles from suspension.

Unsuitable Containers may be taken to include ones made from toxic materials or soft plastics.

Urea An ammonium salt which is suitable for use as a nutrient in place of ammonium phosphate. It is the normal chemical form in which most vertabrates excrete nitrogen waste from their bodies. (Of course, this is not the source of the urea used for this purpose.)

— V —

Vacuum Filtration See Filtration, Vacuum.

Variations in Results are inevitable in winemaking unless careful records are kept and maintained.

Vat The commercial size of cask or tank in which fermentation takes place.

Vegetables A group of ingredients well suited to winemaking where long maturation is anticipated. The chief drawback to their use is that they will require boiling as part of their preparation and therefore the wine is liable to have a high pectin content, unless enzyme preparations are used. In many recipes for the heavier bodied wines, such as sherries or dessert wines, they play an important part in giving the wine its final body.

Vegetables, Preparation of See Boiling Ingredients.

Vigneron The French word for one who grows grapes and makes wines from his fruit.

Vin Ordinaire A class of wine which is not the possessor of a 'label'. Into this class comes most of the 'plonk' that we drink.

Vine The plant from which is obtained the grape.

Vine, Choice of For the British grower, it is best that a white grape-producing plant be chosen. The best choice is made with the advice of the local stockist or vineyard.

Vinegar A word derived from the French, meaning bitter wine. This results from a wine becoming infected with acetomonas or acetobacter. As a result of this, alcohol production ceases and acetic acid is instead produced, with resultant acidity in taste and flavour.

Vinegar Bacteria See Acetobacter; Acetomonas.

Vinegar Fly See Drosophila Melanogaster.

Vinegar Smell The characteristic smell of acetic acid, when present in a wine.

Vineyard A farm or plantation whereon is grown vines for wine production.

Vini Mycoderma (Mycodermi Aceti) See Acetomonas.

Vinification The art of grape production followed by its conversion by fermentation to wine.

Vinometer An inaccurate piece of equipment for measuring the alcohol content of wine. The accuracy is reasonable for totally dry wines, but for sweet wines it is inaccurate, since it works on the principles of surface tension and capillary action.

As a sweet wine has a high surface tension due to the residual sugar, alcohol measurement with a vinometer will give a falsely low reading.

Vinosity A tasting term used to describe the 'wine' taste in an alcoholic beverage.

Vinous Quality, Blending for See Blending for Body.

Vintage In wine drinking circles, it has two meanings. Firstly, it is applied to the year in which the wine is made. Secondly, it is used of such wines as Port and Champagne to indicate wines of a year which is of special greatness. In years which are not declared as vintage, the wine is referred to as non-vintage.

Vintner One who sells wine.

Vitamin Compounds of varying complexity which are essential to life. Most are present in many of the ingredients used for winemaking, with the exception of vitamin B_1. If this is not added to a must, there is a danger that the ferment will stick, since it is needed by the yeast for reproductive reactions. The other vitamins are usually present in sufficient quantities in the ingredients to preclude the need to add them.

Vitamin B_1 See Aneurine Hydrochloride.

Vitamin C See Ascorbic Acid.

Viticulture The art of growing grapes.

Vodka A neutral tasting spirit varying in proof strength from 70% to 140%. It is useful as a fortifying agent. (See Neutral Spirit; Fortification).

Volatile Acidity The part of the total acidity made up of the acids which are driven off at fairly low temperatures. The most important acid in this group is acetic acid. These acids are by-products of fermentation. Their concentration is usually about 0·5 ppt. To estimate the volatile acidity involves distilling a sample of the wine and is therefore beyond the scope of most amateurs.

Volatile Constituents of Wine See Alcohol; Aldehydes; Esters; Volatile Acids; Water.

— **W** —

Washing Soda A caustic cleaning agent which is useful for cleaning stubborn deposits.

Water is a commodity taken very much for granted, but it plays a vital part in winemaking. The professional does not have to rely on tap water, since he only utilises grape juice, but the amateur adds large volumes to the must. The exact role that different water supplies can have on wines is not yet clear.

Water Content of Wine is between 85% and 90% of the total composition.

Water, Gases in All gases normally in air are present in solution in water. For the winemaker, the only one of import is oxygen, which is usually in sufficient quantity to stimulate the yeast to establish a healthy colony. Boiled water does not contain oxygen, so that without aeration the yeast cannot multiply.

Water, Hard is characterised by the presence of calcium and magnesium bicarbonates and sulphates.

Water, Rain Is very soft and, if collected in a country, area, almost sterile (presuming a sterile container). Its use in winemaking must be in conjunction with sufficient magnesium sulphate in the additives to ensure sufficient concentrations of both radicals.

Water, Salts in All water contains chlorides; most water has some nitrogen. (See Water, Hard).

Water, Soft contains little or no calcium or magnesium salts. The latter must be supplied to the ferment as Epsom Salts.

Water and Wine Quality Certainly the presence of magnesium sulphate in hard water will improve a wine. Other than this, little or nothing is known about the effects of local water supplies on wine quality. The only other fact available is that major competitions tend to be won by winemakers from hard water areas. No scientific reasons have been advanced for this as yet.

Weak Acid See Acid, Plant.

Weights and Measures See Appendix XII.

White of Egg See Albumin.

White Turbidity A term for the white haze associated with iron contamination. (See Diagnosis; Haze, Metal; Iron).

White Wine should not show any signs of pinkness, redness or tawny shades in its colour. They tend to be low in tannin, so that they mature quicker than reds. Also, they pass their peak sooner.

White Wine, Range of Colour White is a poor term to use of the colour of a wine. To be more accurate, white wines vary from colourless to pale yellow to amber in colour, and may have a hint of green in them, particularly when young.

Wild Yeasts See Apiculate yeasts; Bloom.

Wine, Classification of is by colour, body, sweetness and style. See Classification of Wine.

Wine, Definition of The *Shorter Oxford Dictionary* defines wine as 'The fermented juice of the grape used as a beverage'. It then goes on to define it as being in wider use, usually with a qualifying word as 'A fermented liquor made from the juice of other fruits or from grain, flowers, the sap of trees, etc'. Thus despite the insistence of many, wine is *not* only made from the grape!

Wine Diseases See Diagnosis, Appendix XI.

Wine, Flowers of See Acetobacter.

Wine Style or Type See Classification of Wines.

Wine Thief A tube with a bulb at one end. The bulb is placed below the surface of a wine to be tasted and when full the open end is occluded by the forefinger. The thief is withdrawn containing a sample of wine. The advantage of using such a piece of equipment is that a wine is little disturbed in sampling.

Wine Yeast See Yeast, Wine.

Wire Ties See Muselet.

Wood Maturing See Cask Maturing.

Woody Taste The taste of a wine stored in a new cask which has not been properly conditioned.

— Y —

Yeast A monocellular organism belonging to the plant kingdom. They are closely related to the fungi. Unlike other plants, fungi and yeasts do not contain chlorophyll and so are unable to utilise sunlight to build up stores of energy (photosynthesis).

Yeast Activity Visible signs of fermentation in a must are the presence of bubbles rising to the surface, together with particles of pulp and clumps of yeast cells.

Yeast, Agar Slope See Agar.

Yeast Autolysis See Autolysis.

Yeast, Bakers' See Bakers' Yeast.

Yeast, Bottom Fermenting A yeast which lies at the base of the fermenting jar. Small clumps of yeast rise to the surface, brought up by the carbon dioxide gas entrapped in them. Wine yeasts are bottom fermenters. Because of this they form compact lees which makes racking easy.

Yeast, Brewers' is taken to be the yeast used by English brewers. It is a top fermenting yeast and forms a thick 'pancake' on top of the fermenting liquor. It gives a rapid ferment and has a lower alcohol tolerance than wine yeasts. If used for a wine, it will confer a beery taste to the wine. Although a bottom fermenting yeast, lager yeast is another species of brewers' yeast.

Yeast Cells are about 5/1,000ths mm in diameter. Their shape can be round, oval or apiculate, depending on the species. The membrane surrounding the cell cannot absorb molecules above a certain size so that, in order to survive, much of their metabolism occurs outside the cell by means of enzymes they secrete. To enable them to do this, they survive best in liquid habitats so that their enzymes may diffuse out and foodstuffs in a utilisable form can diffuse in. They reproduce by budding under ideal conditions, although they are capable of meiosis or binary fission. (See Osmosis).

Yeast, Champagne A species of yeast which is peculiar in that it can continue fermenting under considerable pressures of carbon dioxide which would normally inhibit other wine yeasts.

Yeast Classification There are many genera of yeasts but only the saccharomyces and certain of the spoilage organisms are of import to the winemaker. The saccharomyces (sugar fungus is the translation) are divided into some 30 species of which S. ellipsoideus is the wine yeast; S. cerevisae the beer yeast; S. carlsbergensis the lager yeast. The common spoilage yeasts are the apiculate yeasts of the genus Hanseniaspora; others are Candida and Pichia. The latter is also a constituent of the sherry flor.

Yeast Culture See Culture.

Yeast Deposit   See Deposit; Lees.

Yeast, Dried   One of the main resting forms in which yeast can be purchased. The yeast is encouraged to form spores and then dried gently before packing. In this form, yeast can survive extremes of climate in nature.

Yeast, Feeding   See Exponential Feeding.

Yeast and Fermentation   See Enzyme; Fermentation entries; Appendices IX and X.

Yeast, Film   See Film Yeasts; Pellicle.

Yeast Growth   See Autolysis; Budding; Enzymes; Feeding; Fermentation; Fermentation Pathways, Appendices IX and X.

Yeast Haze   See Haze, Yeast.

Yeast, Liquid Cultures   See Culture.

Yeast for Mead   Most pure wine yeasts are suitable for mead production; the variety recommended would seem to depend on the success of the various authorities.

Yeast Nutrients   See Additives; Ammonium Phosphate; Nutrients; Potassium Phosphates; Vitamin.

Yeast Pitching   The addition of yeast (preferably as an active starter) to a must.

Yeast Preserving   It is possible to keep a yeast culture viable and sterile by careful attention. After preparation of a starter, the culture is allowed to multiply. Once active enough for addition to a must, $\frac{1}{2}-\frac{3}{4}$ is added to the must and the remaining starter is sealed with aseptic techniques. (This involves flaming the bottle neck and stopper.) After this, the sealed bottle is placed in a refrigerator until required again, when it is reactivated by means of another starter solution. Do not keep the sealed bottle in the warm or it will continue to work, with the possible danger of exploding glass.

Yeast, Properties of A good wine yeast will ferment in the presence of a fairly high concentration of alcohol—up to about 16–18% It will form a firm deposit which is not easily disturbed when racked, after a slow steady fermentation. Should the wine be left on the lees, it should not acquire too great a taint from autolysis.

Yeast Reproduction See Binary Fission; Budding.

Yeast, Sherry has a high alcohol tolerance. If maturation is carried out with the wine in contact with air a flor may develope. The bacteriology of this flor would appear to be a complex mixture of sherry yeast, pichia, and acetobacter. The pichia species of yeast are responsible for much of the sherry flavour that developes.

Yeast Starter See Starter.

Yeast Tolerance to Acidity Unlike bacteria and spoilage organisms which are killed or inhibited at a pH of 3·5 or less, yeasts continue to flourish. Indeed, the presence of acid (in particular citric) will ensure the establishment of a healthy ferment.

Yeast, Tolerance to Alcohol See Alcohol Tolerance of Yeast; Yeast, Properties of.

Yeast, Tolerance to Sulphite Yeasts are able to continue fermenting in the presence of sulphur dioxide up to a concentration of about 50 ppm. If greater than this, it is likely that fermentation will be inhibited. To stop fermentation by the addition of sulphite calls for the racking of the wine followed by sulphiting with 50–100 ppm to prevent the establishment of a new colony.

Yeast, Wild See Apiculate Yeasts.

Yeast, Wine Over the centuries each major wine producing area has produced its own variety of S. ellipsoideus by generic mutation. Although taxonomically identical, they do confer slightly different flavours on a wine. *But* the use of a Bordeaux yeast does not mean the automatic production of a Bordeaux style wine. If the must is properly balanced to favour such a wine, the use of such a yeast will enhance these qualities.

Yellow Plastic　See Plastic, Toxic.

— Z —

Zygosaccharomyces　An eponymous name for saccharomyces.

Zymase　The enzyme which catalyses the reduction of acetaldehyde to alcohol. Originally, it was the whole group of fermentative enzymes which were so named. As each enzyme has been isolated and identified, they have been renamed according to their function or structure.

APPENDIX I

Table to convert acidity from one unit to another

from \ to	Citric	Malic	Sulphuric	Tartaric
Citric	—	0·96	0·70	1·07
Malic	1·04	—	0·73	1·10
Sulphuric	1·43	1·37	—	1·53
Tartaric	0·93	0·89	0·65	—

i.e. to convert acidity expressed as ppt citric, to ppt sulphuric multiply by 0·70.

APPENDIX II

Suggested acidities for wine styles

Red	Dry	4·0
	Medium	4·5
	Sweet	5·0
Rosé		5·0
White	Dry	3·0
	Medium	4·5
	Sweet	5·0
	Sparkling	4·5
Dessert	Red	3·0
	White	3·5
Sherry	Dry	2·7
	Sweet	3·3

These values may vary according to taste or the length of maturing anticipated. Longer maturation benefits from increased acidity.

APPENDIX III

Acidity expected from the addition of 7 gm (¼ oz) acid to 1 gallon of wine

Acid	ppt Sulphuric/ Imp. gall.	ppt Tartaric acid/ US gall.
Citric	1·09	1·66
Malic	1·14	1·74
Tartaric	1·02	1·56

APPENDIX IV

Determination of Alcohol Content

a) *By 'original gravity' method.*

Original gravity	Dividing factor	Potential Alcohol	Final SG after complete fermenation
1160	6·82	24·26	994·5
1140	6·87	20·89	996·5
1120	6·93	17·55	998·3
1100	7·00	14·23	1000·35
1080	7·09	10·93	1002·44
1060	7·20	7·67	1004·77
1040	7·39	4·38	1007·63
1020	7·52	1·17	1011·2

Appendix iv—*contd.*

b) *By 'Boiling method'.*

Spirit Indication	Alcohol Content	Spirit Indication	Alcohol Content
1	0·66	14	10·51
2	1·34	15	11·40
3	2·02	16	12·3
4	2·71	17	13·2
5	3·42	18	14·1
6	4·14	19	15·1
7	4·88	20	16·0
8	5·63	21	17·0
9	6·40	22	18·0
10	7·18	23	19·0
11	7·98	24	20·0
12	8·80	25	21·0
13	9·65	26	22·0

The Spirit Indication is the SG of the wine before boiling subtracted from the SG after boiling and reconstituting to its original volume.

APPENDIX V

The relation between Proof° and Alcohol content v/v

Proof°	% Alcohol v/v UK	% Alcohol v/v US
1	0·57	0·5
2	1·15	1·0
3	1·71	1·5
4	2·23	2·0
5	2·86	2·5
10	5·71	5·0
20	11·42	10·0
50	28·50	25·0
100	57·10	50·0

To convert Proof° to Alcohol % v/v:

$$\text{Alcohol \%} = \frac{\text{Proof}° \times 100}{175 \cdot 1}$$

To convert Alcohol % v/v to Proof°:

$$\text{Proof}° = \frac{\text{Alcohol \%} \times 175 \cdot 1}{100}$$

APPENDIX VI

Gravity Tables

Specific Gravity	Gravity	Balling or Brix	Twaddell	Baumé	Weight of Sugar ozs/gal.	gms/l	Potential Alcohol (% by vol)
1.000	0	0.0	0	0.0	½	4	0
1.005	5	1.7	1	0.7	2¾	17	0.8
1.010	10	3.0	2	1.4	4¾	30	1.7
1.015	15	4.3	3	2.1	7	44	2.5
1.020	20	5.5	4	2.8	9	57	3.3
1.025	25	6.8	5	3.5	11	70	4.1
1.030	30	8.0	6	4.2	13¼	83	4.9
1.035	35	9.2	7	4.9	15½	97	5.8
1.040	40	10.4	8	5.6	17½	110	6.5
1.045	45	11.6	9	6.2	19½	123	7.0
1.050	50	12.8	10	6.9	21½	136	8.3
1.055	55	14.0	11	7.5	23¾	149	8.8
1.060	60	15.2	12	8.2	25¾	163	9.6
1.065	65	16.4	13	8.8	28	176	10.4
1.070	70	17.6	14	9.4	30	189	11.2
1.075	75	18.7	15	10.1	32	202	12.0
1.080	80	19.8	16	10.7	34¼	215	12.8
1.085	85	20.9	17	11.3	36½	228	13.6
1.090	90	22.0	18	11.9	38½	242	14.4
1.095	95	23.1	19	12.5	40½	255	15.2
1.100	100	24.2	20	13.1	42¾	268	16.0
1.105	105	25.3	21	13.7	45	282	16.8
1.100	110	26.4	22	14.3	47	295	17.5
1.115	115	27.5	23	14.9	49	308	18.3
1.120	120	28.5	24	15.5	51¼	321	19.1
1.125	125	29.6	25	16.0	53¼	335	19.9
1.130	130	30.6	26	16.6	55½	348	20.7
1.135	135	31.6	27	17.1	57½	361	21.5
1.140	140	32.7	28	17.7	59¾	374	22.2
1.145	145	33.7	29	18.3	62	387	23.0
1.150	150	34.7	30	18.8	64	401	23.8
1.155	155	35.8	31	19.4	66	414	24.6
1.160	160	36.8	32	19.9	68¼	427	25.5

APPENDIX VII

Correction factors for hydrometer readings at various temperatures

Temperature °F	Correction to the *last* figure of the reading obtained
50	subtract 0·6
59	CORRECT
68	add 0·9
77	add 2·0
86	add 3·4
95	add 5·0
104	add 6·8

APPENDIX VIII

Table to calculate sugar additions for sparkling wines from residual sugar content of base wine

Residual Sugar	Add oz/ Imp gall	Add gm/ litre	Add oz/ US gall
0%	2½	15	2
¼%	2	12·5	1½
½%	1½	10	1¼
¾%	1¼	7·5	1
1%	¾	5	½

Residual Sugar Measured by Clinitest

Reading	% Residual Sugar
0%	Blue
¼%	Dark Green
½%	Light Green
¾%	Brown
1%	Khaki
2% or more	Orange

APPENDIX IX

The glycolytic pathway whereby sugars are metabolised to alcohol

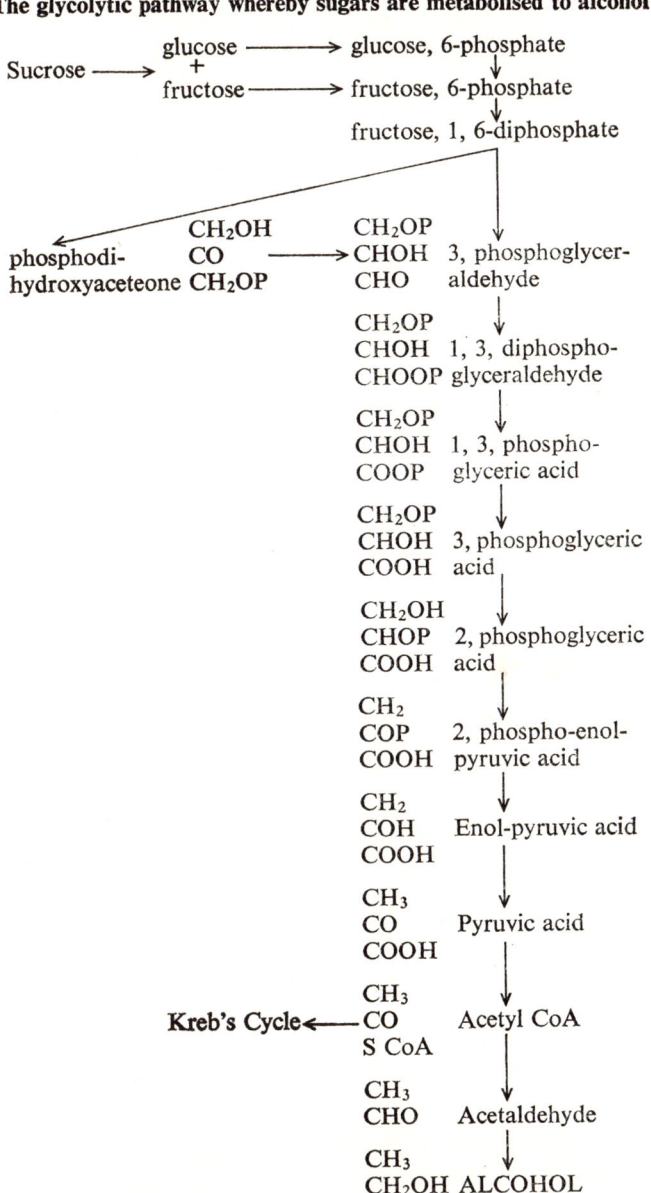

Sucrose → glucose + fructose

glucose → glucose, 6-phosphate

fructose → fructose, 6-phosphate ↓

fructose, 1, 6-diphosphate

phosphodi-hydroxyaceteone
CH_2OH
CO
CH_2OP

→ CH_2OP
$CHOH$
CHO 3, phosphoglyceraldehyde

↓

CH_2OP
$CHOH$
$CHOOP$ 1, 3, diphosphoglyceraldehyde

↓

CH_2OP
$CHOH$
$COOP$ 1, 3, phosphoglyceric acid

↓

CH_2OP
$CHOH$
$COOH$ 3, phosphoglyceric acid

↓

CH_2OH
$CHOP$
$COOH$ 2, phosphoglyceric acid

↓

CH_2
COP
$COOH$ 2, phospho-enol-pyruvic acid

↓

CH_2
COH
$COOH$ Enol-pyruvic acid

↓

CH_3
CO
$COOH$ Pyruvic acid

↓

Kreb's Cycle ← CH_3
CO
$S\ CoA$ Acetyl CoA

↓

CH_3
CHO Acetaldehyde

↓

CH_3
CH_2OH ALCOHOL

APPENDIX X

The metabolic pathway of plant and yeast respiration (The Kreb's cycle)

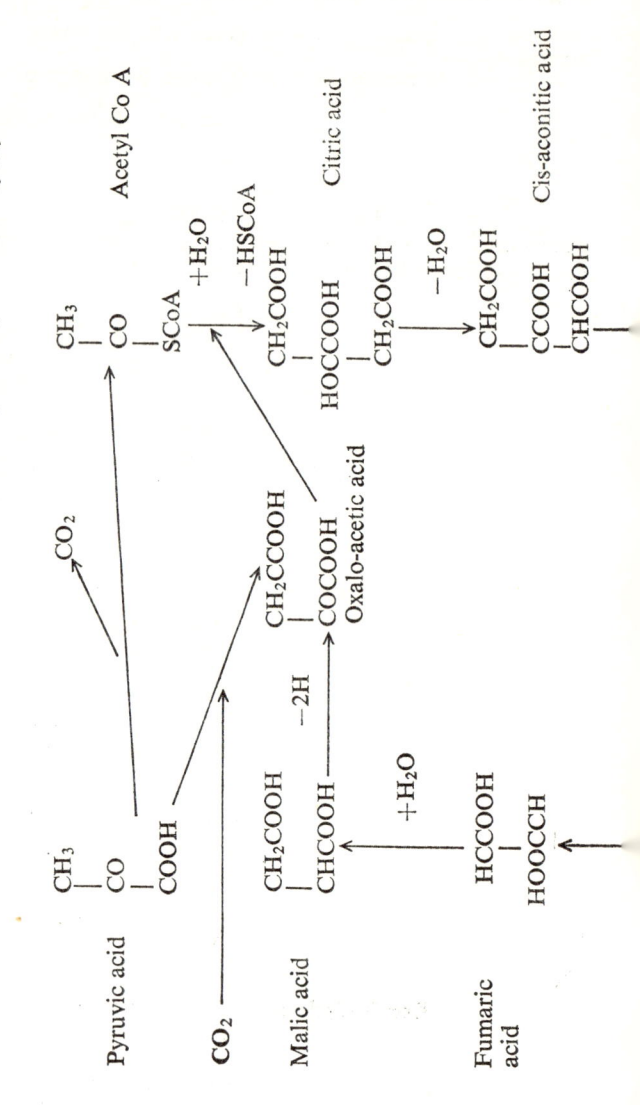

$$CH_3-CO-COOH \quad \text{Pyruvic acid}$$

$$\downarrow CO_2$$

$$CH_3-CO-SCoA \quad \text{Acetyl Co A}$$

$$+H_2O, -HSCoA$$

$$\downarrow$$

$$CH_2COOH-HOCCOOH-CH_2COOH \quad \text{Citric acid}$$

$$\downarrow -H_2O$$

$$CH_2COOH-CCOOH-CHCOOH \quad \text{Cis-aconitic acid}$$

$$CO_2 \rightarrow$$

$$CH_2COOH-CHCOOH \quad \text{Malic acid} \quad \xrightarrow{-2H} \quad CH_2CCOOH-COCOOH \quad \text{Oxalo-acetic acid}$$

$$+H_2O$$

$$HCCOOH-HOOCCH \quad \text{Fumaric acid}$$

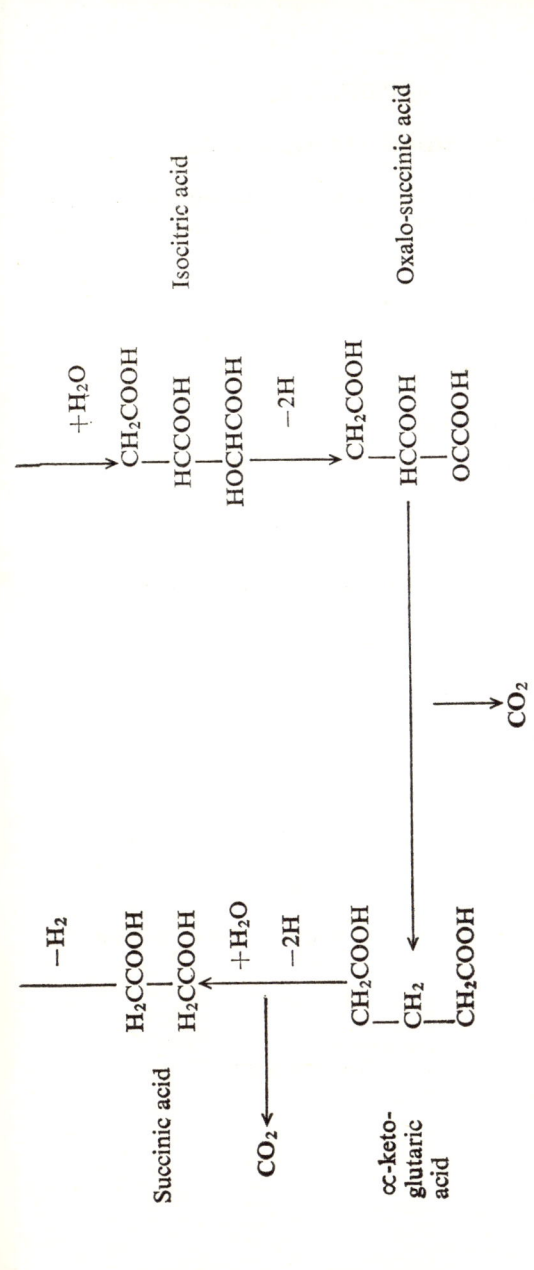

```
                                                    +H₂O
                                                   CH₂COOH
                                                   HCCOOH      Isocitric acid
                                                   HOCHCOOH
                                                    −2H
                                                   CH₂COOH
                                                   HCCOOH      Oxalo-succinic acid
                                                   OCCOOH
                                                       |
                                                       ↓
                                                      CO₂
            −H₂                                        |
           H₂CCOOH                                     ↓
Succinic   H₂CCOOH     CH₂COOH
acid        +H₂O       CH₂
    |       −2H        CH₂COOH
    ↓
   CO₂
α-keto-
glutaric
acid
```

From this series of reactions it can be seen that three of the four acids in common use in winemaking can enter the pathway as shown, or that small amounts of each of these acids will be present in the wine after fermentation has finished. Also, it will be seen that there is a net gain of two molecules of carbon dioxide formed during the cycle. Hence the gas given off during fermentation.

APPENDIX XI

The Diagnosis of Faults in a wine

To use the table, look for the fault in the left-hand column. In the right-hand column is found either the cause or reference numbers for later sections.

Visual Faults

1 Haze or sediment	See 36
2 Patches on surface	Mycoderma infection
3 Skin on surface	
4 Oil on surface	Pre-acetification
5 Wine thicker than usual	Lactobacillus infection
6 'Ropes' in wine	Leuconostoc infection
7 Wine looks like slime	Toropsulosis infection
8 Layering in wine	Wine recently blended. Allow longer ageing
9 Wrong colour for style	See 42

Taste/Smell

10 Smell of bad eggs	Hydrogen sulphide in wine
11 Vinegar	Acetified wine
12 'Tart'	
13 Acetic acid	
14 Peardrops	

15 Mousey	
16 Rancid	Butyric acid bacteria infection
17 Fishy	
18 Burnt	Wine either over-cooked or intended as Madeira type. Charcoal fine if former
19 Caramel	
20 Corked	Cork infection. Discard wine
21 'Swimming bath'	
22 Asbestos	Filter medium not washed before use. Discard wine
23 Cardboard	
24 Paper	
25 Earthy	Wine overfined with Bentonite or dirt from ingredients
26 Yeasty	Young wine. Allow to mature
27 Aldehydic	
28 Astringent	Too much tannin
29 Over or under acid	Reduce with calcium carbonate or Add acid and mature
30 Bitter	Lactobacillus infection with mannitol
31 Cooked	Ingredients boiled too long
32 Prickly	CO_2 still present. Fermenting or malolactic fermentation
33 Musty	Wine on lees too long. Try charcoal

34 Medicinal	Too little acid. Addition has poor chance of improving wine
35 Mousey after taste	Lactobacillus infection

36 Haze with bubbles	See 37
without bubbles	See 39
37 SG falling	Active ferment. Continue
SG static	See 38
38 Acidity falling	Malo-lactic ferment
Acidity static	Secondary ferment
39 SG 1020 or more	Stuck ferment (see entries)
SG 1020 or less	See 40
40 Haze with sediment	See 41
Haze without sediment	See test entries to find cause
41 Wine recently racked	See test entries
Wine not recently racked	Rack and reassess after 3 months
42 Wine meant to be red	See 43
white	See 44
Rosé	See 45
43 Wine too dark	Too long on pulp, or too much fruit
Wine too pale	Not enough pulp ferment, or too little fruit
44 Wine too dark	See tests
Wine too light	Not enough fruit

45 Wine too dark   Too long on pulp

   Wine too light   Not enough pulp ferment

   Orange tint in wine   Poor blend of red and white

46 Brown colour in wine   If sherry or dessert wine—correct

                          If white wine—oxidation

APPENDIX XII

Weights and Measures.

These tables give approximate equivalents. They are not intended for absolute accuracy, but rather for ease of use. To avoid lengthy tables only values of common usage in winemaking are given.

a) **Weight**

Metric (*Grams*)	Imperial (*Ounces*)
1	1/30
2	$\frac{1}{15}$
7	$\frac{1}{4}$
10	$\frac{1}{3}$
15	$\frac{1}{2}$
30	1
115	4
225	8
450	16 (1 lb)
1000 (1 kilo)	36 (2¼ lb)

b) **Fluid**

Metric ml.	Imperial Pints	Imperial Oz.	U.S.A. Pints	U.S.A. Oz.
1		1/30		1/30
7		$\frac{1}{4}$		$\frac{1}{4}$
10		$\frac{1}{3}$		$\frac{1}{3}$
15		$\frac{1}{2}$		$\frac{1}{2}$
30		1		1
140	($\frac{1}{4}$)	5		5
285	($\frac{1}{2}$)	10		10
570	1		1	4
4500	8 (1 gal)		10	

c) Spoon Sizes

Approximate measures of the common spoon sizes.

Fluid ozs.	Metric	U.K.	U.S.A.
$\frac{1}{60}$	½ml.	Salt spoon	
$\frac{1}{15}$	2ml.	Egg spoon	
$\frac{1}{8}$	4ml.	Coffee spoon	Tea spoon
$\frac{1}{6}$	5ml.	Tea spoon	
$\frac{1}{3}$	12ml.		Table spoon
$\frac{1}{2}$	15ml.	Dessert spoon	
$\frac{5}{6}$	25ml.	Table spoon	Serving spoon

d) Temperature

Fahrenheit°	Centigrade°
32	0
50	10
55	12
60	15
70	20
80	27
212	100

REFERENCES

When compiling a book such as this, it is impossible not to use hundreds of references. Those of particular value and interest are listed:

Amateur Winemaker (Magazine)
Amateur Winemaking, S. M. Tritton (Faber 1971)
Biochemistry for Medical Students, W. V. Thorpe (Churchill 1960)
Calculating Alcohol Yields, W. Honneyman (Semplex Home Brew 1966)
Customs and Excise Act 1952, H.M.S.O.
Encyclopaedia of Wines & Spirits, A. Lichine (Cassell 1967).
Etudes sur le Vinaigre, L. Pasteur (1868)
First Steps in Winemaking, C. J. J. Berry (*Amateur Winemaker*)
General and Inorganic Chemistry, P. J. Durrant (Longmans 1956)
Gravity Tables, H.M.S.O.
How to make Wines with a Sparkle, J. Restall and D. Hebbs (*Amateur Winemaker* 1972)
Introduction to Organic Chemistry, Fieser & Fieser (Heath & Co., Boston 1957)
Journal of Alcoholism
Judging Home-made Wines and Beers, A.W.N.G.J. (*Amateur Winemaker* 1971)
Making Mead, G. W. B. Acton and P. M. Duncan (*Amateur Winemaker* 1972)
Making Wines Like Those You Buy, Duncan and Acton (*Amateur Winemaker* 1971)
Liqueurs, Aperitifs and Fortified Wines, B. Olney (Foremost 1972)
Penguin Book of Home Brewing and Winemaking, W. H. T. Tayleur (Penguin 1973)
pH Values and Their Determination, British Drug House (1970)
Plant Form and Function, F. E. Fritsch and E. Salisbury (Bell & Son 1957)
Progressive Winemaking, Duncan and Acton (*Amateur Winemaker* 1971)
Science and Technique of Wine, L. Frumkin (Lea & Co. 1965)
Science of Wine, C. Austin (U.L.P. 1968)

Scientific Winemaking Made Easy, J. R. Mitchell (*Amateur Winemaker* 1969)
Spirit Tables, H.M.S.O.
Technology of Winemaking, Amerine and Creuse
Testing Wines, A. M. Tuckett and K. V. J. Hockings (Grey Owl Laboratory)
Vegetable, Herb and Cereal Wines, T. E. Belt (Foremost 1971)
Whys and Wherefores of Winemaking, C. Austin (*Amateur Winemaker*)
Winemaking and Brewing, F. W. Beech and A. Pollard (*Amateur Winemaker* 1971)
Winemaker's Companion, B. C. A. Turner and C. J. J. Berry (Mills & Boon 1971)
World Atlas of Wines, H. Johnson (Mitchell, Beasley 1972)